T0301909

An Analysis of

Theodore Levitt's

Marketing Myopia

Elizabeth Mamali
With
Monique Diderich

Published by Macat International Ltd
24:13 Coda Centre, 189 Munster Road, London SW6 6AW.

Distributed exclusively by Routledge
2 Park Square, Milton Park, Abingdon, Oxon OX14 4RN
711 Third Avenue, New York, NY 10017, USA

Routledge is an imprint of the Taylor & Francis Group, an informa business

www.macat.com
info@macat.com

Cataloguing in Publication Data
A catalogue record for this book is available from the British Library.
Library of Congress Cataloguing-in-Publication Data is available upon request.
Cover illustration: Etienne Gilfillan

ISBN 978-1-912302-16-1 (hardback)
ISBN 978-1-912127-33-7 (paperback)
ISBN 978-1-912281-04-6 (e-book)

Notice
The information in this book is designed to orientate readers of the work under analysis,
to elucidate and contextualise its key ideas and themes, and to aid in the development
of critical thinking skills. It is not meant to be used, nor should it be used, as a
substitute for original thinking or in place of original writing or research. References and
notes are provided for informational purposes and their presence does not constitute
endorsement of the information or opinions therein. This book is presented solely for
educational purposes. It is sold on the understanding that the publisher is not engaged
to provide any scholarly advice. The publisher has made every effort to ensure that
this book is accurate and up-to-date, but makes no warranties or representations with
regard to the completeness or reliability of the information it contains. The information
and the opinions provided herein are not guaranteed or warranted to produce particular
results and may not be suitable for students of every ability. The publisher shall not be
liable for any loss, damage or disruption arising from any errors or omissions, or from
the use of this book, including, but not limited to, special, incidental, consequential or
other damages caused, or alleged to have been caused, directly or indirectly, by the
information contained within.

CONTENTS

THE MACAT LIBRARY

The Macat Library is a series of unique academic explorations of seminal works in the humanities and social sciences – books and papers that have had a significant and widely recognised impact on their disciplines. It has been created to serve as much more than just a summary of what lies between the covers of a great book. It illuminates and explores the influences on, ideas of, and impact of that book. Our goal is to offer a learning resource that encourages critical thinking and fosters a better, deeper understanding of important ideas.

Each publication is divided into three Sections: Influences, Ideas, and Impact. Each Section has four Modules. These explore every important facet of the work, and the responses to it.

This Section-Module structure makes a Macat Library book easy to use, but it has another important feature. Because each Macat book is written to the same format, it is possible (and encouraged!) to cross-reference multiple Macat books along the same lines of inquiry or research. This allows the reader to open up interesting interdisciplinary pathways.

To further aid your reading, lists of glossary terms and people mentioned are included at the end of this book (these are indicated by an asterisk [*] throughout) – as well as a list of works cited.

Macat has worked with the University of Cambridge to identify the elements of critical thinking and understand the ways in which six different skills combine to enable effective thinking.
Three allow us to fully understand a problem; three more give us the tools to solve it. Together, these six skills make up the **PACIER** model of critical thinking. They are:

ANALYSIS – understanding how an argument is built
EVALUATION – exploring the strengths and weaknesses of an argument
INTERPRETATION – understanding issues of meaning

CREATIVE THINKING – coming up with new ideas and fresh connections
PROBLEM-SOLVING – producing strong solutions
REASONING – creating strong arguments

To find out more, visit **WWW.MACAT.COM.**

CRITICAL THINKING AND "MARKETING MYOPIA"

Primary critical thinking skill: PROBLEM SOLVING
Secondary critical thinking skill: CREATIVE THINKING

Theodore Levitt's 1960 article "Marketing Myopia" is a business classic that earned its author the nickname "the father of modern marketing". It is also a beautiful demonstration of the problem solving skills that are crucial in so many areas of life – in business and beyond.

The problem facing Levitt was the same problem that has confronted business after business for hundreds of years: how best to deal with slowing growth and eventual decline. Levitt studied many business empires – the railroads, for instance – that at a certain point simply shrivelled up and shrank to almost nothing. How, he asked, could businesses avoid such failures?

His approach and his solution comprise a concise demonstration of high-level problem solving at its best. Good problem solvers first identify what the problem is, then isolate the best methodology for solving it. And, as Levitt showed, a dose of creative thinking also helps. Levitt's insight was that falling sales are all about marketing, and marketing is about knowing your real business. The railroads misunderstood their real market: they weren't selling rail, they were selling transport. If they had understood that, they could have successfully taken advantage of new growth areas – truck haulage, for instance – rather than futilely scrabbling to sell rail to a saturated market.

ABOUT THE AUTHOR OF THE ORIGINAL WORK

Born in Germany in 1925, **Theodore Levitt** and his family relocated to Dayton, Ohio, in the United States when he was 10. He received his doctorate in economics from Ohio State University and began his teaching career at the University of North Dakota. Levitt then joined the Harvard Business School in 1959 and taught there until he retired in 1990. He also worked as a consultant to businesses, especially in the oil industry. He and his wife of 58 years had four children. Dubbed "the father of modern marketing," Levitt died in 2006.

ABOUT THE AUTHORS OF THE ANALYSIS

Dr Elizabeth Mamali is a lecturer in marketing at the School of Management, University of Bath. Her work focuses on social theory and qualitative social research. Her most recent publication is "Mobilizing hegemonic practices in trajectories of conspicuous resistance."

Dr Monique Diderich holds a masters degree in psychology from the University of Groningen and a doctorate in sociology from the University of Nevada, Las Vegas. She now holds a position at the University of Maryland

ABOUT MACAT

GREAT WORKS FOR CRITICAL THINKING

Macat is focused on making the ideas of the world's great thinkers accessible and comprehensible to everybody, everywhere, in ways that promote the development of enhanced critical thinking skills.

It works with leading academics from the world's top universities to produce new analyses that focus on the ideas and the impact of the most influential works ever written across a wide variety of academic disciplines. Each of the works that sit at the heart of its growing library is an enduring example of great thinking. But by setting them in context – and looking at the influences that shaped their authors, as well as the responses they provoked – Macat encourages readers to look at these classics and game-changers with fresh eyes. Readers learn to think, engage and challenge their ideas, rather than simply accepting them.

'Macat offers an amazing first-of-its-kind tool for interdisciplinary learning and research. Its focus on works that transformed their disciplines and its rigorous approach, drawing on the world's leading experts and educational institutions, opens up a world-class education to anyone.'

Andreas Schleicher
Director for Education and Skills, Organisation for Economic
Co-operation and Development

'Macat is taking on some of the major challenges in university education … They have drawn together a strong team of active academics who are producing teaching materials that are novel in the breadth of their approach.'

Prof Lord Broers,
former Vice-Chancellor of the University of Cambridge

'The Macat vision is exceptionally exciting. It focuses upon new modes of learning which analyse and explain seminal texts which have profoundly influenced world thinking and so social and economic development. It promotes the kind of critical thinking which is essential for any society and economy.
This is the learning of the future.'

Rt Hon Charles Clarke, former UK Secretary of State for Education

'The Macat analyses provide immediate access to the critical conversation surrounding the books that have shaped their respective discipline, which will make them an invaluable resource to all of those, students and teachers, working in the field.'

Professor William Tronzo, University of California at San Diego

WAYS IN TO THE TEXT

KEY POINTS

- The business scholar Theodore Levitt was born in Germany in 1925 and moved to the United States when he was 10 years old.

- His 1960 article "Marketing Myopia" made him famous as "the father of modern marketing."

- Levitt analyzed why businesses suffer from slowed or zero growth; for him, it is important that any business should put the customer first.

Who Was Theodore Levitt?

Theodore Levitt, the author of the article "Marketing Myopia" (1960), was born in Germany in 1925. When he was 10 years old, his family relocated to the United States, settling in Dayton, Ohio. He interrupted his high school education to fight in World War II* for the Americans in Europe. After the war, he finished high school through a correspondence course and worked as a sportswriter for a newspaper in his hometown in Ohio.

Eventually, Levitt obtained a doctorate in economics at Ohio State University and began his academic career as an assistant professor at the University of North Dakota. His early writings attracted the attention of both business—mostly leaders of oil companies—and academia. In 1959 the prestigious Harvard Business School at Harvard

University in Cambridge, Massachusetts, invited him to join its faculty. Levitt also served as a consultant for the giant corporation Standard Oil,* among other oil companies.

Although he published many articles and books during his tenure at Harvard Business School, his 1960 article "Marketing Myopia" made him world-famous. At the time Levitt published this landmark article, marketing did not even exist as a separate discipline in business. This influential article secured his reputation as "the father of modern marketing." Levitt was also the first to popularize the term "globalization," by which he meant that technology would erode the differentiation of consumer needs in markets around the world. After a long and fruitful career, Levitt retired from Harvard Business School in 1990. Levitt and his wife had four children. They had been married for 58 years when he died in 2006.

What Does "Marketing Myopia" Say?

Theodore Levitt wondered how businesses that once thrived could see their growth slow or stop altogether. Recognizing that companies went out of business when the market for their products dried up, Levitt embarked on a journey to analyze how this occurred.

He found that companies had too narrow a definition of the business they were in. For example, film producers in Hollywood were in the movie industry, so they produced movies. When television became the primary source of entertainment in American households, the movie industry felt threatened, worrying that TV would make people less inclined to visit movie theaters. But Levitt says if movie companies had defined themselves as being in the entertainment business, they would have recognized television as just another way to distribute their product.

In another industry, Levitt examines the once-thriving railroad companies. It may seem clear to us that these companies were in the business of transportation. But railroad companies defined themselves much more narrowly, missing the opportunity to carry greater numbers of goods and people that were otherwise transported by, say, buses or trucks. As the population of the United States grew substantially after World War II, one might have expected to see a corresponding growth in railroad companies as they transported more products and more people. That this did not happen can be attributed to the railroad companies' failure to understand correctly the nature of their business.

Levitt also shows what could go wrong with the growth of oil companies. In his day, cars and trucks depended solely on gasoline, a product of oil. Customers had to buy gasoline regularly—but Levitt notes that customers do not like to refuel their cars, finding it a nuisance. When a company comes along and invents another source of fuel, he pointed out, oil companies will lose business and their growth will slow or stop. To prevent that from happening, he thought that oil companies should invest in exploring alternative sources of energy; not only would they develop another income stream independent of gasoline, they would also demonstrate their willingness to put their customers first.

Levitt emphasizes the importance of making the customer central to a company's business plan. He urged organizations to think about what the customer wants and needs—revolutionary advice at a time when companies focused on their products rather than on their customers; the consensus was that if products were good enough they would sell themselves, and if they did not sell themselves, then advertisements would sell them.

Levitt noticed that many companies remained too focused on the product and its advertising and that focusing on the customer produces much better results for a business. No matter how good a product may be, if a potential customer does not believe in it, the customer will not buy it. People will not buy products they do not like or need—and no amount of advertising can change that. The solution, Levitt argues, is for a company to focus on the customer and not on the product.

Why Does "Marketing Myopia" Matter?

Levitt wrote "Marketing Myopia" as a manifesto, intending it to serve as a wake-up call for management practitioners, using straightforward—even blunt—language to engage his readers. Although Levitt's ideas were not entirely new, his clear writing style enabled him to reach a wide audience. Levitt also provided examples from real-world businesses so managers could relate to his argument. Nearly 1,000 businesses in the United States purchased reprints of the article when it was first published. Managers wanted to know how they might prevent their business from losing customers.

Levitt also attracted attention from the academic community. Scholars saw his work as groundbreaking because he so clearly articulated the notion of putting the customer first. "Marketing Myopia" sparked the development of marketing as an academic field—one reason Levitt earned the title of "the father of modern marketing." As marketing has blossomed as an academic discipline, Levitt's writings remain staples of the curriculum in management and business schools.

The ideas Levitt articulates in this article still resonate with scholars and business managers today, who have built on his notion of a customer-centric orientation. Today, technology enables organizations to enlist their customers as collaborators. Some companies' websites allow customers to tailor products to their unique preferences; companies selling athletic footwear were among the first to take advantage of this trend.

Levitt's notion of putting the customer first led to the development of the concept of "relationship marketing."* The idea is that developing relationships with customers enhances customer retention. A customer with a strong relationship, that is, will continue to buy goods or services from that particular company, enabling the company to grow and prosper.

"Marketing Myopia" remains a timeless classic. Scholars and business leaders agree that many ideas Levitt put forward more than 50 years ago still provide insights into business today.

SECTION 1
INFLUENCES

MODULE 1
THE AUTHOR AND THE
HISTORICAL CONTEXT

KEY POINTS

- Born in 1925 in Germany, Theodore Levitt moved to the United States at the age of 10. As a young man, he fought with the US Army in World War II.*

- During his lifetime, Levitt witnessed major technological innovations that changed the ways businesses produced their goods.

- He based his influential article "Marketing Myopia" on an astute analysis of what makes businesses fail or thrive.

Why Read This Text?

In his 1960 article "Marketing Myopia," Theodore Levitt suggests that businesses succeed when they focus on satisfying customers' needs rather than on selling products alone. Businesses whose sales strategy is oriented toward products assume that superior products are sufficient to attract customers. So instead of worrying about retaining existing customers—and developing new ones—these businesses preoccupy themselves matters such as the cost-benefits of mass production (the savings they can make, in time and production costs, by automated manufacturing on a large scale). In doing so, Levitt says they exhibit "myopia"—that is, nearsightedness.

Levitt argues that companies suffering from myopia do not focus on the evolving, long-term needs of the market. Assuming their products will sell themselves, they become oblivious to changes in customers' desires. This orientation toward products allows competitors outside the industry to develop and offer products that satisfy consumers more effectively than existing offerings.

❝ Every major industry was once a growth industry. But some that are now riding a wave of growth enthusiasm are very much in the shadow of decline. ❞
Theodore Levitt, "Marketing Myopia"

In Levitt's view, businesses that fail to adapt to consumers' needs will eventually become obsolete and go out of business. To avoid extinction, companies must develop a customer orientation:* the prioritization of the consumer's needs as the starting point and main drive behind their business activities. This key change will allow companies to define their markets in ways that accurately reflect what their customers want.

Scholars and businesspeople considered "Marketing Myopia" revolutionary when it was published. In fact, it marks the beginning of the modern marketing movement and has become a classic text. The Harvard Business School Publishing Corporation has reissued it as a standalone booklet, most recently in 2008.

Author's Life

Theodore Levitt was born in Germany in 1925 to working–class parents who decided to leave Germany after Adolf Hitler* gained power in 1933 and the extreme right–wing Nazi Party* started to dominate German life. When Levitt was 10 years old, he and his family moved to the United States and settled in Dayton, Ohio. Drafted by the US Army during World War II, Levitt left high school to fight in Europe. After the war, he completed high school through a correspondence course, while also working as a sportswriter for the Dayton *Journal Herald* newspaper.[1] Levitt graduated from Antioch College* and earned a doctorate in economics from Ohio State University* in 1951. He began his teaching career at the University of North Dakota.* His 1956 article "The Changing Character of

Capitalism," published in the *Harvard Business Review,** "caught the eye of the Standard Oil Company* and resulted in him becoming a much sought-after consultant to the oil and other industries for the next phase of his career."[2] He relocated to Harvard Business School* in 1959 and worked there until his retirement in 1990. He died in 2006.

Harvard Business Review published Levitt's influential article "Marketing Myopia" in 1960. Its arguments—revolutionary for the time—remain relevant for many kinds of businesses more than 50 years later. Some 1,000 businesses ordered more than 35,000 reprints of the article in the first weeks after its publication. To date, the article has sold nearly 900,000 copies.[3]

Theodore Levitt published 26 articles in *Harvard Business Review*, making him one of the journal's most prominent authors; in 1985, he became its editor. During his four-year tenure he made the academic journal accessible to a large readership, including top business leaders, by running shorter articles about a wider range of subjects—and even humorous, *New Yorker*-style cartoons.[4]

Author's Background

Theodore Levitt came of age in the United States of the 1940s and 1950s. During World War II, many of the nation's women worked in factories affiliated with the war industry, while the men fought in Europe and the Pacific. In the 1940s, factories all over the US adopted assembly lines, enabling mass production of goods; automating production spurred substantial business growth. After the war ended, many people in the United States felt so optimistic about the state of the world that they started having more children. This started the first wave of the baby boom generation:* children born between 1946 and 1964 would comprise the largest generation the United States had ever seen—and, in business terms, an affluent market of considerable size; during the 1950s, the standard of living rose in the United

States—people no longer needed their entire paycheck just to pay for food and housing. They were able to purchase a car, a family home, and household appliances and even go on the occasional family vacation.

As the American middle class grew, individuals and families became consumers. More American households bought televisions, which further promoted consumerism through advertisements interspersed in the black-and-white broadcasts—color TVs were still some years away. Americans were coming to see themselves in a new light—as consumers. Levitt believed companies needed to see these consumers in a new light as well, to capture and retain their business.

At that time, as Levitt noted, business saw "marketing" as a synonym for "selling." Companies would look for strategies to sell more of their products and services. They had little regard for what customers really wanted and were not concerned with building long-term relationships with their clients. Levitt's article "Marketing Myopia" redefined marketing, producing lasting changes in the ways businesses relate to their customers.

NOTES

1   Jan Bailey, "Profile on Theodore Levitt: the Father of Modern Marketing," *Engineering Management* 16 (2006): 48–9.

2   Bailey, "Profile on Theodore Levitt," 48.

3   Barnaby J. Feder, "Theodore Levitt, 81, Who Coined the Term 'Globalization,' Is Dead," The *New York Times*, July 6, 2006, accessed November 7, 2015, www.nytimes.com/2006/07/06/business/06levitt.html.

4   Harvard University Gazette, "Professor Theodore Levitt, Legendary Marketing Scholar and Former Harvard Business Review Editor, Dead at 81," *Harvard University Gazette* July 20, 2006, accessed November 7, 2015, http://news.harvard.edu/gazette/2006/07.20/99–levitt.html.

MODULE 2
ACADEMIC CONTEXT

KEY POINTS

- Theodore Levitt was influenced by his contemporaries in the United States—in particular, the management scholar Peter F. Drucker,* who had already emphasized the importance of a business being customer-oriented.

- During Levitt's lifetime, American consumers became more prosperous and American businesses turned to techniques of mass production.

- Levitt's influential article "Marketing Myopia" made him one of the founders of the discipline of modern marketing.

The Work in its Context

In "Marketing Myopia," Theodore Levitt discusses the effect that mass production had on business. In his lifetime, he watched the growth of large enterprises that used relatively novel technology, such as the assembly line, in which a product is put together piece by piece by different workers or machines, exponentially to increase production of goods and services. These goods traveled coast to coast on the US railroad system, whose companies also grew as railroads became the major mode of transportation for freight. Passengers flocked to railroads, too. When people wanted to travel long distances in the 1920s, 1930s, and 1940s, trains were their best (indeed, for many people their only) option.

However, eventually the railroad business stopped growing—and not because the need to transport freight and passengers declined. In fact, Levitt saw demand for transportation increasing. So he set out to analyze what happened to the railroad business, and to other businesses that suffered a similar decline.

> **❝ Mass production industries are impelled by a great drive to produce all they can. ❞**
> Theodore Levitt, "Marketing Myopia"

Levitt intended "Marketing Myopia" to serve as a manifesto. He wanted his bold arguments to challenge how corporations define their business. His approach was not original—as Levitt himself acknowledges. A number of business scholars had already conducted marketing work of a similar nature. But unlike those previous authors, Levitt used concise, easily accessible language. He illustrated his arguments with real-life examples of businesses that had once thrived, such as the railroads, and analyzed why they had withered or failed. He made such convincing arguments that business students still read his article more than a half-century later.

Overview of the Field

The field of marketing matured and expanded during the 1950s and 1960s. Even before Levitt wrote his article, American business schools had started to take note of marketing practices. Scholars and businesspeople alike began to question the prevailing focus on products and started to shift their thinking toward a focus on consumers; the emphasis shifted, that is, to the demonstration of how products might solve customers' problems. In this context, we may see "Marketing Myopia" as the product of Levitt's observation of the ways corporations conducted business.

Another reason to become customer-orientated at the time stemmed from the fact that the 1950s and 1960s saw the growth of a consumer culture in American society. The US standard of living increased substantially during the 1950s. As a result, the middle class expanded, which meant more customers buying American manufacturers' goods and services. Customers bought things they needed, of course, but also things they perceived as symbolizing prosperity and social status. This cultural environment created conditions in which companies were freer than ever before to define their businesses according to what consumers wanted. "Marketing Myopia" pointed the way forward, and suggested a harsh fate for those who lagged behind the trend.

Academic Influences

Theodore Levitt was primarily influenced by his contemporaries, including the American business and management scholars Wroe Alderson,* Neil Borden,* and Peter F. Drucker. While not formal members of a clearly distinguished intellectual movement, Drucker, Borden, and Alderson belonged to the generation of academics that built the foundations of modern marketing concepts.

Alderson took an interdisciplinary approach to marketing and earned a reputation as one of the most important marketing theorists of the twentieth century. Borden, Levitt's colleague on the Harvard Business School faculty, made significant contributions to the practice of advertising management. Specifically, he introduced the innovative concept of "marketing mix,"* a strategic marketing tool aimed at four key marketing areas: product, price, place, and promotion.

Peter F. Drucker straddled the worlds of academia and business, as Levitt would. He spent more than 50 years teaching management at graduate-school level and served as a consultant for large corporations such as General Motors, IBM, and General Electric. Drucker's works, including *Concept of the Corporation*[1] and *The Practice of Management,*[2] influenced Theodore Levitt's scholarship. In 1975, Levitt specifically mentioned Drucker as one who had provided him with a "great deal of insight."[3] He particularly cited Drucker's work on the concept of marketing. In *The Practice of Management,* published six years before Levitt wrote "Marketing Myopia," Drucker posed three simple questions: What is our business? Who is our customer? What does our customer consider valuable? Drucker claimed that "business has two functions—marketing and innovation."[4] This sparked debate and led managers and academics to pay attention to the business theory.

The Harvard professor and distinguished economist John Kenneth Galbraith* was also an influence. Galbraith's 1958 book *The Affluent Society*[5] focused on creating consumer demand for products through advertising. Galbraith, in turn, was influenced by the American economist Thorstein Veblen.* In his book *The Theory of the Leisure Class*[6] Veblen coined the term "conspicuous consumption"* to describe the spending patterns of people who consume goods to make a statement of their wealth and display their social status. Veblen had been talking about wealthy people; by the time Levitt wrote "Marketing Myopia," the newly prosperous American middle class had begun to adopt this behavior as well.

Levitt viewed advertising as an artificial creation of wants:[7] a way of making people believe they want something that they do not really need. He saw Galbraith as being product-oriented: pushing and selling the product to consumers. As Thorstein Veblen* puts it, Levitt "denied that marketing was a nefarious way of 'separating consumers from their loose change' and contended instead that customers come first, last and always."[8]

NOTES

1   Peter F. Drucker, *Concept of the Corporation* (New York: Day, 1946).

2   Peter F. Drucker, *The Practice of Management* (Oxford: Butterworth-Heinemann, 1955).

3   Theodore Levitt, "HBR Classic: Marketing Myopia," *Harvard Business Review* September–October (1975): 180.

4   Neharika Vohra and Kumar Mukul, "Relevance of Peter Drucker's Work: Celebrating Drucker's 100th Birthday," *Vikalpa* 34 (2009): 2.

5   John Kenneth Galbraith, *The Affluent Society* (Boston, Mass.: Houghton Mifflin, 1958).

6   Thorstein Veblen, *The Theory of the Leisure Class* (Auckland: Floating Press, 1899).

7   Colin Grant, "Theodore Levitt's Marketing Myopia," *Journal of Business Ethics* 18 (1999): 397–406.

8   Stephen Brown, "Reconsidering the Classics: Reader Response to 'Marketing Myopia,'" *Journal of Marketing Management* 21 (2005): 474.

MODULE 3
THE PROBLEM

KEY POINTS

- Levitt examined businesses in a variety of industries that experienced slowed or zero growth.
- He advocates a marketing perspective focused on the consumer, not the product.
- Levitt's views became widely accepted within the emerging discipline of marketing.

Core Question

In "Marketing Myopia," Theodore Levitt focuses on once-thriving businesses that had stopped growing, looking at several different business sectors to see if the businesses in them whose growth had slowed or stopped exhibited any common characteristics.

In each sector, he asks key questions such as: Which businesses prosper and why? Which businesses suffer from slowed or stopped growth? What role does management play in each of those businesses? How does management define the company's business? Who are their customers?

Levitt recognized that his findings would be of interest primarily to managers in the field. The few studies that had already been published catered mainly to an academic audience, but, knowing his own customer base, he understood that business managers were eager for some way to analyze and understand the forces that seemed to be conspiring to take down their once-prosperous enterprises. So rather than write in the style of the complex and lengthy academic works that inspired his own inquiry, Levitt wrote an article that was short

> ❝ Mass production does indeed generate great pressure to 'move' the product. But what usually gets emphasized is selling, not marketing. ❞
> Theodore Levitt, "Marketing Myopia"

enough for busy executives actually to read and accessible enough for managers to be able to understand exactly how significant these insights were.

To ensure that he would grab the attention of businesspeople, Levitt wrote his article as a manifesto and included real-life examples from a variety of business sectors, so managers of many different organizations could relate to his arguments.

The Participants

When Levitt wrote his article, businesses assumed that their superior products would sell themselves to consumers who had increased their standard of living during the 1950s. Businesses viewed advertising as a way to encourage those consumers who might need a little bit of persuasion. The discipline of marketing was in its infancy, with academics such as John Kenneth Galbraith* and Neil Borden* focused on advertising strategies aimed at separating consumers from their money.[1] The only academic in the field advocating that businesses should focus on their customers rather than their products was Peter F. Drucker.*[2] So Levitt's theories stood virtually alone.

In "Marketing Myopia," Levitt examined a diverse array of industries: the railroads, the oil and petroleum industry, the automobile industry, and the movie industry. Businesses in each of these industries faced challenges due to changes in society—primarily from technological inventions and the newly expanding consumer market.

When television became mainstream in the 1950s, the movie industry in Hollywood felt threatened; movie producers worried that people would visit theaters less often. But producers were clinging to a very narrow definition of their product. If they had seen themselves as producing entertainment rather than just movies, they might have embraced the expansion of their market to television. Instead, as Levitt observes, "all the established film companies went through drastic reorganizations."[3] Young writers, producers, and directors with a track record of successfully producing for television saved Hollywood's film industry from becoming obsolete.

The once-thriving railroad industry faced a similar fate. Those companies also defined their business too narrowly. While they saw themselves as being in the railroad business, they would have done better to define themselves as being in the transportation business. Goods and people can be transported by means other than railroad, such as buses or trucks, but because the railroad companies defined their business narrowly, they neglected this option. Levitt notes that "as transporters, the railroads still have a good chance for very considerable growth."[4] He considers this the difference between a product orientation and a consumer orientation.

People who drive cars find refueling them a big nuisance. But despite what gasoline companies think their product is, Levitt says that when consumers go to a gas station, they simply pay for "the right to continue driving their cars."[5] That "right to continue driving" can come from gasoline—or from some substitute that had yet to be invented when Levitt wrote "Marketing Myopia." Although the new product did not yet exist, the farsighted company that developed it would provide the solution consumers crave: eliminating the need for frequent trips to the gas station. Companies that invent such solutions will thrive because "they are satisfying a powerful customer need."[6]

The Contemporary Debate
Immediately after its publication, "Marketing Myopia" sparked the interest of many businesses and thousands of reprints were ordered.[7]

Levitt's suggestions promised to help them break free of the slowdown gripping many American businesses in the era. If the ideas in this journal article could help them avoid slowing their growth—and potentially stay in business—then companies were prepared to make changes. But companies did not suddenly embrace the consumer out of the goodness of their hearts. They were interested in growth, and if that meant paying attention to the customer and looking for alternate products, then they would embrace those tactics. For example, oil companies realized they needed to look for alternate sources of energy to stay in business. They chose coal and started buying coalmines.[8]

Within academia, some scholars remained focused on product-oriented marketing. The marketing scholar Neil Borden developed different elements to market products to consumers. He remained product-oriented, and saw advertising as central to marketing the product. In his 1967 book *Marketing Management: Analysis, Planning, and Control*[9] Philip Kotler* helped popularize a classification of four main areas of marketing—the product, its price, its placement, and its promotion ("the 4 Ps."). The idea was that these four areas, when properly adapted, would be instrumental in satisfying customers.

NOTES

1   John A. Quelch and Katherine E. Jocz, "For the Greater Goods," *The American: A Magazine of Ideas*, November–December (2008): 72–7.

2   Neharika Vohra and Kumar Mukul, "Relevance of Peter Drucker's Work: Celebrating Drucker's 100th Birthday," *Vikalpa* 34 (2009): 1–7.

3   Theodore Levitt, "Marketing Myopia," *Harvard Business Review* July–August (1960): 45.

4   Levitt, "Marketing Myopia," 46.

5   Levitt, "Marketing Myopia," 53.

6   Levitt, "Marketing Myopia," 53.

7   Barnaby J. Feder, "Theodore Levitt, 81, Who Coined the Term 'Globalization,' Is Dead," The *New York Times*, July 6, 2006, accessed November 7, 2015, www.nytimes.com/2006/07/06/business/06levitt.html.

8   John Kay, "Sometimes the Best that a Company can Hope for is Death," The *Financial Times*, August 21, 2013, accessed November 25, 2015, http://www.johnkay.com/2013/08/21/sometimes-the-best-that-a-company-can-hope-for-is-death.

9   Philip Kotler, *Marketing Management*: *Analysis, Planning, and Control* (Englewood Cliffs, NJ: Prentice-Hall, 1967).

MODULE 4
THE AUTHOR'S CONTRIBUTION

KEY POINTS

- Levitt makes a distinction between marketing (a customer-oriented approach) and selling (a product-oriented approach).
- Levitt wrote his article as a manifesto to attract readers from the business world.
- The article generated significant interest across the business world and in academia.

Author's Aims

In "Marketing Myopia," Theodore Levitt aims to demonstrate why once-thriving businesses experienced slowed or stopped growth. He has three intentions. The first is to define an important problem in the market that affected businesses across many industries; the second is to identify and detail the causes of that problem; finally he aims to provide solutions to remedy the problem.

Taking a closer look at those aims, Levitt wanted managers to understand the reasons growth had slowed in their respective sectors and he wanted to demonstrate how a change in marketing approach—prioritizing the consumer over the product—could reverse that slowdown. He intended the article to be a declaration of his strong views that could serve as a "wake-up call" for businesspeople. Levitt wanted to appeal to his audience very directly, knowing that "the colorful and lightly documented affirmation works better than the torturously reasoned explanation."[1]

The structure of the article accurately reflects Levitt's aims. Basing his argument on case studies, Levitt draws examples from sectors

❝ Selling focuses on the needs of the seller, marketing on the needs of the buyer. **❞**

Theodore Levitt, "Marketing Myopia"

ranging from grocery stores and gas stations to automobile manufacturers and the movie business. He analyzes these cases and draws theories from them to find the roots of the slowdown. He finds that product-oriented companies suffer from slowed or stopped growth. They may even become obsolete, if customers stop buying their products. Levitt also engages the reader by indicating precisely how a consumer-oriented market approach could safeguard growth. So Levitt did not just identify problems; he offered solutions.

Levitt makes no claim that his ideas are new; he acknowledges the influence of Wroe Alderson,* Neil Borden,* and Peter F. Drucker.* He views his own contribution as tying "marketing more closely to the inner orbit of business policy."[2] He intended his article as "merely … a simple, brief, and useful way of communicating an existing way of thinking."[3]

Approach

"Marketing Myopia" includes case studies of several different industries: the film industry, the automobile industry, the railroad industry, the oil and petroleum industry, and the grocery store industry. All these industries focused on making their products, assuming that consumers would buy them without the inducement of marketing. But Levitt observes that their actual market is the consumer buying the product, not the product itself.

To appreciate the author's aims, today's readers need to consider the conditions of the era in which Levitt wrote "Marketing Myopia." After World War II,* rapid technological progress created product innovations; mass production allowed manufacturers to turn out their products in record numbers. And increases in disposable income drove an increase in consumer spending. Products practically flew off the shelves, so how could managers not assume that their superior, technologically advanced products needed little help from "marketing"? Why should they spend valuable time and money investigating who buys the products, or why? Product-oriented marketing seemed to work exceptionally well—for a time. Then companies found their growth slowing, even as the overall market grew. Levitt's advice to focus on what consumers wanted went against what businesspeople of the time had observed or been taught. The message truly was revolutionary.

Contribution in Context

Levitt's use of real-world case studies legitimized his argument in the eyes of the business world. This was not just some proclamation from the ivory tower of academia; this was a serious examination of what was actually happening in American business. Levitt's provocative writing style, his efficient and direct way of addressing his target audience, captured the attention of managers in a range of industries. With nearly 35,000 reprints of the article sold in the first month after its publication,[4] "Marketing Myopia" prompted managers to reconsider the way they market their products and address their consumers.

Yesterday's revolutionary thinking has become today's conventional wisdom. We now take for granted the message of "Marketing Myopia." And that may be the best compliment paid to Levitt's work. Businesses have reassessed their marketing approach; customer-orientation has become routine. If this has not happened as a direct result of Levitt's work, we may certainly attribute it to something the author himself predicted: "If an organization does not know or care where it is going ... everybody will notice it soon enough."[5]

Managers who were focused on the superiority of their products failed to see that they risked obsolescence by not recognizing consumers' needs. But when Levitt pointed out the problem with this way of thinking, businesses took notice. Levitt not only upended conventional ways of thinking about marketing, he did so in a work that remains a classic—even though the conditions that sparked it have long disappeared. The views Levitt presents have become widely accepted in business and provide a solid foundation for contemporary academics to research.

In 1999, Theodore Levitt told an interviewer that he had intended "Marketing Myopia" as a manifesto: "I said, Look at what you're doing … Look at what business you're in. Define your business in a way that liberates you to do the things that you have to do, can do, will need to do, given what people want: It was designed to be a statement of the possibilities."[6]

NOTES

1 Theodore Levitt, "HBR Classic: Marketing Myopia," *Harvard Business Review* September–October (1975): 181.

2 Levitt, "HBR Classic: Marketing Myopia," 180.

3 Levitt, "HBR Classic: Marketing Myopia," 180.

4 Jan Bailey, "Profile on Theodore Levitt: the Father of Modern Marketing," *Engineering Management* 16 (2006): 48.

5 Theodore Levitt, "Marketing Myopia," *Harvard Business Review* July–August (1960): 56.

6 Jeffrey M. O'Brien, "Drums in the Jungle," *MC: Technology Marketing Intelligence* 19 (1999): 24.

SECTION 2
IDEAS

MODULE 5
MAIN IDEAS

KEY POINTS

- Theodore Levitt analyzed why businesses become obsolete.

- He identified four myths top managers believed about business practices and pointed them toward the truth about their businesses.

- Using clear language and examples drawn from actual companies, Theodore Levitt succeeded in communicating his message to management practitioners and the academic community.

Key Themes

In "Marketing Myopia," Theodore Levitt explores what he considered myths surrounding the business culture. If managers believe in them, those myths will ultimately harm and threaten the continued success of their business. He advises managers to focus on their consumers instead of on their products—whether goods or services.

Levitt analyzes how a customer orientation could help formerly thriving companies return to health. He saw that companies get into trouble when they ignore customer needs. Managers define their business incorrectly, or too narrowly, when they focus only on their products rather than on the people who buy them. In other words, being extremely product-oriented makes them shortsighted or myopic.

Levitt begins his analysis with the problem of obsolescence—the state in which companies find themselves when consumers desert

> **❝** It is all too easy in this day and age for a company or industry to let its sense of purpose become dominated by the economies of full production and to develop a dangerously lopsided product orientation. **❞**
>
> Theodore Levitt, "Marketing Myopia"

them. That notion seems inconceivable to managers focused on the presumed superiority of their product. Smugly assuming that their product alone will ensure a steady stream of loyal customers, they fail to notice that consumers' needs change. So they do not develop new products to address those changing needs, much less create new products to serve as-yet-unrecognized needs. Eventually, this resistance to adapting renders their products obsolete. Customers—and profits—disappear and another once-thriving business closes its doors.

Exploring the Ideas

Levitt identifies what he calls a "self-deceiving cycle of bountiful expansion and undetected decay"[1] in "the history of every dead and dying 'growth industry.'"[2] He attributes that cycle to four main conditions.

First, managers were convinced that a growing population, which was also more affluent, would guarantee consumers for their products. Levitt wrote his article after World War II,* when unprecedentedly high birth rates in the United States were creating what came to be known as the baby boom generation.* Levitt argues that if managers think their company's product has an automatically growing market they "will not give much thought to how to expand it."[3] Levitt wryly summarizes the issue: "If thinking is an intellectual response to a problem, then the absence of a problem leads to the absence of thinking."[4]

Second, top managers believed that consumers would not be able to find a substitute for the product or service they sell. That led individual companies to focus exclusively on improving their current product rather than on innovating. Meanwhile, other companies may develop novel products that reduce the demand for existing products, or even render them obsolete. Levitt provides the example of the oil industry confining itself to "oil exploration, production, and refining,"[5] leaving outsiders such as the motor vehicle manufacturer General Motors* and the giant chemical company DuPont* to develop tetraethyl lead, an additive to gasoline that increased fuel economy. While the additive is no longer used in the United States because of its toxicity, at the time this represented a major leap forward for the oil industries. Similarly, natural gas replaced the oil used to heat many households, reducing consumer demand for oil.

Third, business leaders put too much faith in mass production. It is easy to see how this can happen; when companies automate their production process, output increases and product costs decline. As Levitt explains, "The profit possibilities look spectacular. All effort focuses on production with the result that the marketing gets neglected."[6] Companies focus on selling their product—a one-sided action. Company leaders just assume that the consumer wants what their business produces. They do not engage with buyers to find out what they actually want or need. Marketing, however, involves advertising the benefits of the product and building relationships with potential consumers.

Fourth, managers remain too preoccupied with improving their product, while reducing the cost of manufacturing it. Although automobile companies spent millions of dollars on consumer research, they did not ask open-ended questions that would allow consumers to give voice to their needs. In this way, Levitt notes, they failed to acknowledge what consumers really wanted. It never occurred to industry leaders that customers wanted something different from what they were already getting. As a result, the American automobile industry, centered in Detroit, "lost millions of customers to other small-car manufacturers."[7] As Levitt notes, "Detroit never really researched customers' wants. It only researched their preference between the kinds of things it had already decided to offer them. For Detroit is mainly product oriented, not customer oriented."[8]

Language and Expression

"Marketing Myopia" had a profound impact on American business. It grabbed the attention of managers in general and marketing practitioners in particular. But then, Levitt had targeted "Marketing Myopia" at professionals rather than scholars. Instead of complex academic language, he writes in a straightforward, assertive tone more likely to catch a practitioner's attention. His style bridges the gap between theory and practice—something many academic writers struggle to do.

Businesspeople have applauded Levitt's engaging writing style: "Levitt is a leading academic authority in a leading academic institution, yet he manages to portray himself convincingly as a practical man, an ordinary Joe, one of the guys."[9] Another critic described the article as "short, punchy, and largely citation-free … For many practicing managers, Theodore Levitt is more than a skillful advocate of the marketing cause; he *is* marketing."[10]

An Irish scholar compares Levitt to the ancient Celtic bards, who communicated by telling stories: "Storytelling," he notes, "is central to marketing ideology,"[11] adding that Levitt has taught marketing scholars "the importance of writing, and writing well."[12]

NOTES

1   Theodore Levitt, "Marketing Myopia," *Harvard Business Review* July–August (1960): 57.

2   Levitt, "Marketing Myopia," 57.

3   Levitt, "Marketing Myopia," 48.

4   Levitt, "Marketing Myopia," 48.

5   Levitt, "Marketing Myopia," 48.

6   Levitt, "Marketing Myopia," 50.

7   Levitt, "Marketing Myopia," 51.

8   Levitt, "Marketing Myopia," 51.

9   Stephen Brown, "Marketing and Literature: the Anxiety of Academic Influence," *Journal of Marketing* 63 (1999): 5.

10 Brown, "Marketing and Literature," 5.

11 Aedh Aherne, "Exploit the Levitt Write Cycle," *Journal of Strategic Marketing* 14 (2006): 77.

12 Aherne, "Exploit the Levitt Write Cycle," 86.

MODULE 6
SECONDARY IDEAS

KEY POINTS

- When companies pay too much attention to research and development,* they narrow their focus too much.

- It is rare that top managers engage in systematic exploration using scientific methods.

- Product-oriented* businesses may lose existing customers and have a difficult time appealing to potential new consumers.

Other Ideas

In "Marketing Myopia," Theodore Levitt notes that businesses can focus too much on technical research and development (R&D). They do this believing that any new product they develop will be so superior—like their existing products—that it will sell itself. Companies focused on R&D tend to hire executives with a background in engineering, but no matter how long they have been in management, these professionals remain first and foremost scientists.

Scientists running businesses tend to see the product as more important than the customer. Products can be tested, reduced to sets of data points, and analyzed; customers cannot. People are generally driven by needs and wants, not by data and facts. The engineer-manager may believe that the company's skilled sales force, armed with a superior product, can sell the customer anything. But time and again, as Levitt points out, the market has proved these engineer-managers wrong.

While engineer-managers may pride themselves on being fact-based and data-driven, Levitt notes that scientists in top management

> **❝ Another big danger to a firm's continued growth arises when top management is wholly transfixed by the profit possibilities of technical and research development. ❞**
> Theodore Levitt, "Marketing Myopia"

become "totally unscientific when it comes to defining their companies' overall needs and purposes."[1] These scientists abandon the scientific method when it comes to selling products. They do not focus on identifying the company's problems. They do not develop testable hypotheses aimed at solving those problems. Levitt writes they "are scientific only about the convenient things, such as laboratory and product experiments."[2]

Exploring the Ideas

The secondary ideas Levitt raises in "Marketing Myopia" build on his key themes, particularly the problem of obsolescence and its remedy (the adoption of a customer orientation). Managers focus narrowly on research and development—which seems to be a safe path, especially for those trained as scientists. But that path may lead to a company's demise. The road to success passes through the dangerous-sounding process Levitt calls "creative destruction."[3] Levitt means that companies need to break loose from the ways in which they traditionally operate. No product should be considered above elimination—even a core product, if it can be replaced with one that better satisfies customers' needs. Levitt states that, for their own good, the oil firms will have to "destroy their own highly profitable assets. No amount of wishful thinking can save them from the necessity of engaging in this form of 'creative destruction.'"[4]

Levitt does not equivocate, boldly writing, "the historic fate of one growth industry after another has been its suicidal product provincialism."[5] By "product provincialism," Levitt means defining the product in too narrow terms. For example, in his view the oil and petroleum industry should focus on developing a replacement for automobile fuel so motorists do not have keep going to the gas station to refuel their cars. The creative destruction of the need for gasoline would reduce the industry's profits from the fuel's sale. But that would be more than offset by profits from the new fuel source. And that new product would also better meet their customers' needs.

When companies allow themselves to become obsessed with technical research and development, managers come to see their product as a superior product that will sell automatically. This perspective makes them shortsighted (myopic)—unable to see consumers' real needs. Levitt cautions against a "philosophy that continued growth is a matter of continued product innovation and improvement."[6] He sees R&D as "the greatest danger" to a company's continued existence.[7]

Levitt illustrates his argument with a story from the electronics industry, an industry whose success was fueled by military subsidies and orders. The military was receptive to the new technology, so the products sold themselves. Levitt writes that the electronics companies' "expansion has, in other words, been almost totally devoid of marketing effort."[8] This is an enviable position—but it creates the dangerous illusion that all a company needs in order to grow is a steady supply of superior products. If the industry's client base changed, it would find itself in trouble without a marketing strategy to attract and retain new customers.

Overlooked

"Marketing Myopia" focuses entirely on discussing a single topic: the problem of slowed or stopped growth in industries. Shifting a company to a consumer orientation can, according to Levitt, provide a useful solution to this problem. Given this singular focus, we cannot say that any particular aspect of the article has been overlooked.

Theodore Levitt's work enhanced the business practices in the latter half of the twentieth century—and his principles continue to be followed today. He argued that industries should redefine their sectors according to customer needs. And he warned that if they did not shift their orientation, they risked becoming obsolete. While not neglected, the concept of obsolescence has received considerably less attention from academics and practitioners. This may stem from the fact that readers of business works remain more likely to focus on the author's suggested solutions, rather on the conditions that rendered a solution necessary. The good news is that developments in the marketing field—some spurred by Levitt's analysis—will likely prevent managers from repeating the mistakes of their 1950s and 1960s counterparts.

A recent article with the provocative title "Sometimes the Best that a Company can Hope for is Death" disagreed with Levitt's view. Rather than fight obsolescence, this scholar suggests companies should accept it as a natural part of the business cycle. If a company does not have a competitive advantage, we should not be surprised when it becomes obsolete.[9]

Although the cultural context in which businesses operate has seen major changes since Levitt wrote his article more than a half-century ago, his observations have proven to be timeless, precisely because we may look at his argument from different angles and reinterpret it to reflect the current state of markets.

NOTES

1   Theodore Levitt, "Marketing Myopia," *Harvard Business Review* July–August (1960): 55.

2   Levitt, "Marketing Myopia," 55.

3   Levitt, "Marketing Myopia," 53.

4   Levitt, "Marketing Myopia," 53.

5   Levitt, "Marketing Myopia," 53.

6   Levitt, "Marketing Myopia," 54.

7   Levitt, "Marketing Myopia," 53.

8   Levitt, "Marketing Myopia, "54.

9   John Kay, "Sometimes the Best that a Company can Hope for is Death", *The Financial Times*, August 21, 2013, accessed November 25, 2015. http://www.johnkay.com/2013/08/21/sometimes-the-best-that-a-company-can-hope-for-is-death.

MODULE 7
ACHIEVEMENT

KEY POINTS

- The corporation needs to focus on satisfying its customers. Businesses have widely adopted Levitt's concept of customer orientation.*

- Since no two industries face the same challenges, they cannot benefit from the same analyses; companies producing industrial products benefited more from Levitt's advice than consumer product companies.

- Some businesses still suffer from myopia— shortsightedness—if they fail to focus on the needs and wants of their customers.

Assessing the Argument

In "Marketing Myopia," Theodore Levitt argues that a business does not begin with a product, a raw material, a patent, or a skill. It begins with the customer. "In order to produce these customers, the entire corporation must be viewed as a customer-creating and customer-satisfying organism."[1] Levitt wants to inspire business leaders focused on product above all to adopt a more consumer-oriented perspective.

Levitt constructs an argument that could apply to many sectors. His message: To battle generational shifts in consumers' wants and technological advancements, companies must stop defining themselves solely (or even primarily) by their product or service. They should focus on the needs that a product or service actually satisfies. Whether looking at challenges facing the dry cleaning industry, electric utilities, grocery stores, or Hollywood studios, Levitt's analysis offers a widely effective remedy.

❝ The view that an industry is a customer-satisfying process, not a goods-producing process, is vital for all business people to understand. ❞
Theodore Levitt, "Marketing Myopia"

Levitt does not seek to prescribe sector-specific tactics. Instead, he offers strategic direction about how to confront a phenomenon that affected a range of industries at the time. Just as he does not intend his arguments for only one industry, Levitt also does not intend his arguments to challenge only one part of a company. He is not writing for marketing departments, the area traditionally responsible for communicating the company's message to markets. He wants to reach—and change the thinking of—executives across all of a company's business functions.

Achievement in Context
Perhaps one reason Theodore Levitt's message reached so many areas of the business world is that it could apply to so many disparate industries. Hollywood studios refocused themselves as sellers of entertainment and even lifestyles, rather than just movies. And businesses applied Levitt's central arguments on a smaller scale, too, using them to inform everything from advertising campaigns to product design.

Today, the messages in "Marketing Myopia" have become part of basic marketing theory. But that does not mean that myopia no longer exists in the business world. The nearsightedness Levitt identified still manifests itself whenever an organization neglects to prioritize its consumers' needs. For example, the snack food company SunChips manufactures a whole-grain alternative to the potato chip. In an attempt to capitalize on sustainability and promote "green thinking," the brand launched environmentally friendly packaging in 2010. But the new packaging turned out to be very noisy, and consumers rejected it. By ignoring the impact that noisy packaging would have on its customers, SunChips exhibited signs of the myopia Levitt addressed in 1960.[2]

"Marketing Myopia" carries a timely and timeless message. In the years before Levitt wrote it, developments in mass production and technology had boosted supply and the cultivation of a consumer culture had significantly enhanced demand. Companies across all industries experienced growth, almost without lifting a finger. That dynamic changed as consumers began to exercise their power of choice. Levitt helped business leaders identify the disconnection between their product-centric practices and consumers' changing needs. Levitt's sophisticated marketing advice helped them focus more on consumers, which forever changed the ways in which products were marketed.

One other important note: Levitt, an esteemed scholar, published his marketing "manifesto" in a distinguished academic journal at a time when academia did not hold business in particularly high esteem. "Marketing Myopia" did not just change how business viewed marketing, it also changed how academia viewed business. Levitt legitimated the discipline of marketing as an area of study and it remains a staple in business schools to this day.

Limitations

While Levitt's work suggests that all sectors can benefit from his solutions, the arguments he makes remain highly industry-dependent. Critics have often accused him of taking a "one size fits all" approach by defining the problem of obsolescence in the same terms for all companies. Levitt neglects to analyze whether individual differences (such as bad management or market particularities) could be responsible for slowed or stopped growth.

Similarly, his central argument about customer orientation does not apply equally to all sectors. Fifteen years after the article's initial publication, Levitt himself recognized that industrial-product companies benefit significantly more from his advice than their counterparts in other sectors. And consumer-product companies needed his advice less, since they already focused on their consumers.[3]

Aside from being industry-dependent, Theodore Levitt's manifesto is also time-dependent. All marketing treatises share this limitation, because the social and cultural environment significantly affects how companies market their goods. In 1960, when "Marketing Myopia" was published, the discipline of marketing remained relatively new. It had not yet been fully accepted as a legitimate social science in American and European business schools.

The post-World War II* consumers Levitt addressed differed significantly from their successors in our era. While yesterday's consumers did not look for much beyond a great product or service, today's want great products surrounded by a compelling story or myth. For example, the rebellious image of the Harley Davidson motorcycle brand attracts people who want more than the utility of driving a motorcycle. The brand represents an entire lifestyle—people buy the Harley culture as much as they do its bikes.

Today, some companies also get customers involved in creating product. Internet technology allows customers to customize the items they purchase, creating their own unique product. For example, different companies offer consumers the opportunity to build a bicycle from the ground up and customize apparel from business suits to sportswear and athletic shoes. Product customization* creates brand loyalty.[4]

Developments in consumerism—in the sense of a focus on the consumer's wants and needs—and the evolution of more sophisticated marketing techniques do not lessen the importance of Theodore Levitt's arguments. A customer orientation remains important. But his half-century-old arguments do not always address the sociocultural demands of today. Despite these criticisms, in its original context "Marketing Myopia" offered a fresh perspective for managers on how to approach the consumers in their markets.

NOTES

1   Theodore Levitt, "Marketing Myopia," *Harvard Business Review* July–August (1960): 56.

2   Jacquelyn Ottman and Mark Eisen, "Green Marketing Myopia and the SunChips Snacklash," *Harvard Business Review Blog Network* (2010), accessed December 7, 2013, http://blogs.hbr.org/2010/10/green-marketing-myopia-and-the/.

3   Theodore Levitt, "HBR Classic: Marketing Myopia," *Harvard Business Review* September–October (1975): 26–8, 33–4, 38–9, 44, 173–4, 176–81.

4   Elizabeth Spaulding and Christopher Perry, "Making it Personal: Rules for Success in Product Customization," *Bain Insights Newsletter*, September 16, 2013, accessed November 23, 2015, http://www.bain.com/publications/articles/making-it-personal-rules-for-success-in-product-customization.aspx.

MODULE 8
PLACE IN THE AUTHOR'S WORK

KEY POINTS

- Throughout his career, Levitt argued that companies have a responsibility to determine and meet the needs of their consumers.

- A customer orientation should be a holistic (that is, integrated or cohesive) part of business operations — not just a strategy employed by a marketing department.

- Levitt inspired practitioners as well as scholars. He helped to further develop marketing as an academic field while communicating his ideas in a way that businesspeople could connect with.

Positioning

In "Marketing Myopia" and most of his other works, Theodore Levitt raised the idea that industries should gear their operations around customers' needs. This is one of the many arguments that bind together Levitt's body of work.

In his book *Marketing for Business Growth* (1974),[1] Levitt extends the ideas he raised in "Marketing Myopia." He develops a visual tool he calls a "marketing matrix."* The matrix both measures the marketing orientation of companies and analyzes how well they meet their customers' key requirements. In his journal article "The Globalization* of Markets" (1983)[2]—one of his many works published in *Harvard Business Review*—Levitt argues that technological advances have changed the nature of business, homogenizing markets (making them internally similar) and bringing them together.

> **❝** To the extent that the customer is recognized as having needs that the manufacturer should try to satisfy, Detroit usually acts as if the job can be done entirely by product changes. For Detroit is mainly product oriented, not customer oriented. **❞**
>
> Theodore Levitt, "Marketing Myopia"

In a globalized market, Levitt believes companies will do better if they focus on offering a standardized product that is superior in design, reliability, and price. While the notion of globalization has become commonplace today, many people credit Levitt as being among the first to use the term and bring it into common discourse. The "Globalization" article and "Marketing Myopia" have several common qualities. Both share the manifesto style of writing, and both analyze real-world case studies. But by 1983 the arguments in "Marketing Myopia" had become generally accepted, so Levitt uses "The Globalization of Markets" to go further. He suggests that companies are not just responsible for learning what customers want—they must understand even more about customers' needs than the customers themselves can articulate. Finally, Levitt's last book, *Thinking about Management* (1991),[3] revisits the arguments of "Marketing Myopia" as well as many of the other theories the author developed during his long and distinguished career.

Integration

Levitt's arguments in "Marketing Myopia" reflect the influence of other management scholars of the time who engaged with similar ideas. The scholar and business consultant Peter F. Drucker* argued in his acclaimed 1954 work *The Practice of Management* that a company's primary responsibility remains serving its customers.[4] This idea underpins Levitt's theme of customer orientation.* In 1957—three years before Levitt wrote "Marketing Myopia"—the marketing theorist Wroe Alderson* described firms as ecological systems. Alderson saw marketing activity as facilitating interaction among different functions within the company.[5] Levitt also tended to approach businesses as holistic entities. In "Marketing Myopia" he describes how adopting a customer orientation requires participation from executives across all functions of the business, not just the marketing managers.

Alderson also argued that "goods do not really have utility from the consumer viewpoint until they come into the possession of the ultimate user and form a part of his assortment."[6] Alderson's value-in-use* concept (the various benefits customers enjoy by consuming a particular product or service) and Levitt's later discussion of customer orientation both focus on how products can satisfy customers.

If one can argue that the ideas in "Marketing Myopia" predate Levitt's work, he certainly provided a fresh perspective by extending these ideas and revealing new implications for business. Levitt also illustrates his themes with real-world case studies. This is one of his work's greatest attributes. He examines a range of industries, showcasing examples of good and bad practices to support his claims. In that way he frames the concept of customer orientation, setting it in the context of an existing problem—the slowed or stopped growth of industries; his argument that companies need to define their businesses in customer-oriented terms extended and enhanced existing thinking on the subject.

Significance

The impact of Levitt's work was felt by "literally thousands of organizations throughout the United States, the UK and worldwide."[7] Both scholars and practitioners have heaped extensive praise on "Marketing Myopia." Many see it as having made a significant contribution to the rise of modern marketing in the 1960s. It also legitimized the discipline in business schools in the United States and Europe.

The work also influenced Levitt's contemporaries. For example, Peter F. Drucker revisits ideas from "Marketing Myopia" in his 1964 book *Managing for Results*.[8] Drucker argues that businesses should not approach marketing analysis as ordinary market research but should, rather, investigate the market, the customers, their spending patterns, their purchases, and their motivation for buying certain products.[9] Drucker suggests, as Levitt had, that the way customers use products should become the driving force behind a company's operations.

Levitt also popularized the concept of globalization*— increasingly close political, cultural, and economic ties across continental boundaries. In his 1983 article "The Globalization of Markets," he wrote that markets all over the world share a key attribute: "the one great thing all markets have in common is an overwhelming desire for dependable, world-standard modernity in all things, at aggressively low prices."[10]

His work has influenced people all over the world. In particular, his articles "Marketing Myopia" and "The Globalization of Markets" have been translated into many languages and featured in business-related anthologies. Levitt remains celebrated as one of the most influential management gurus.[11] By developing the concept of customer orientation* and evaluating relationship marketing* as a key tool for businesses (as he does in his 1983 book *The Marketing Imagination*) he has created a lasting legacy. He gave businesses the marketing tools they need to succeed in the modern world.

NOTES

1   Theodore Levitt, *Marketing for Business Growth* (New York: McGraw-Hill, 1974).

2   Theodore Levitt, "The Globalization of Markets," *Harvard Business Review* May/June (1983): 98.

3   Theodore Levitt, *Thinking About Management* (New York: Free Press, 1991).

4   Peter F. Drucker, *The Practice of Management* (New York: Harper & Row, 1954).

5   Wroe Alderson, *Marketing Behavior and Executive Action: A Functionalist Approach to Marketing Theory* (Homewood IL: Richard D. Irwin, 1957).

6   Alderson, *Marketing Behavior and Executive Action,* 70.

7   Jan Bailey, "Profile on Theodore Levitt: the Father of Modern Marketing," *Engineering Management* 16 (2006): 48.

8   Peter F. Drucker, *Managing for Results* (New York: Harper & Row, 1964).

9   Drucker, *Managing for Results*.

10 John A. Quelch and Katherine E. Jocz, "For the Greater Goods," *The American: A Magazine of Ideas,* November–December (2008): 76.

11 Sultan Kermally, "Theodore Levitt," in *Gurus on Marketing* (London: Thorogood, 2003), 43–56.

SECTION 3
IMPACT

MODULE 9
THE FIRST RESPONSES

KEY POINTS

- When it was first published, "Marketing Myopia" was praised by scholars and management practitioners, who considered the article innovative and revolutionary.

- Critics questioned whether Levitt's ideas could really apply universally and whether his case studies were good representations of the business sectors he studied.

- In 1975, Levitt responded, updating the original article with comments, and published it again in the journal *Harvard Business Review.**

Criticism

More than five decades after its original publication, Theodore Levitt's "Marketing Myopia" has proven to be a timeless work. It has had significant impact on both business and academia, with leaders in both worlds praising it highly. For decades—at least until Levitt's death in 2006—people generally accepted his main argument, that companies should move away from a product orientation* to focus on consumers. However, nothing remains immune to criticism forever and challenges have arisen.

In "Marketing Myopia," Levitt relied heavily on the use of real-life case studies to define the problem of obsolescence. Managers have found this approach particularly useful because it gives them a window into how their peers handled challenges. But some critics have argued that the case-study approach ignores the differences between business sectors. Each industry has its own individual characteristics; no two markets behave alike. Further, some charge that the case studies Levitt

> **❝** In order to produce these customers, the entire corporation must be viewed as a customer-creating and customer-satisfying organism. **❞**
>
> Theodore Levitt, "Marketing Myopia"

selected may not be the best representations of each specific business sector he addresses. And even within the same sector, companies' growth slows or stops for different reasons.

Some have noted that many of the industries that the author criticized for their product orientation have managed to survive—and even to grow—decades after the publication of "Marketing Myopia." These include Hollywood studios and the oil industry. We might see this as an illustration that Levitt's "one size fits all" approach does not reflect the realities of doing business. One critic recently argued that companies do not need to imagine what business they are in; they need to keep a competitive edge over their competition.[1]

One other criticism raised against Levitt involved his views of the economist John Kenneth Galbraith's* perspective on advertising, Galbraith believed that advertising created artificial desires in potential customers. Levitt clearly distinguished between selling the product and marketing to the consumer. In his view, selling focuses on the needs of the seller, while marketing focuses on the needs of the consumer. But one critic argued in 1999 that Levitt basically did advocate selling—though perhaps in a more sophisticated form.[2]

Responses

Perhaps as an indirect response to some of these critiques, Levitt wrote a commentary on the work 15 years after "Marketing Myopia" first appeared. In this article, also published in *Harvard Business Review*, Levitt offers specific examples of how his work had a dramatic impact on businesses. For example, oil companies shifted their thinking to being in the "energy business," which drove them to explore new ventures such as coal. Levitt illustrates how sensitivity to customer needs has led businesses from shoe retailers to glass companies to grow in volume, earnings, and return on assets.[3]

While Levitt's core argument remained the same, in this retrospective he focuses on its real-world impact. He recognizes that customer orientation* has proven to be a lot more helpful for industrial product companies than consumer product companies. The latter already focused on customers; their business always depended on it.

Levitt also expands on the conditions that lead to obsolescence. He discusses how factors specific to companies could have slowed their growth. For example, he acknowledges that chief executives with a purely economic or finance background remain less able to understand the diversities of the market and so less open to the idea of catering to smaller market segments. These executives assume that profits can only be made when reaching mass markets. Despite these refinements in his argument, Levitt's views remained mostly intact. As he wrote in the 1975 commentary: "Of course, I'd do it again and in the same way, given my purposes, even with what more I now know."[4]

Conflict and Consensus

Despite the validity of critics' arguments, the consensus view remains that "Marketing Myopia" remains a "marketing classic."

The noted academic and marketing guru Peter F. Drucker* supported Levitt's argument that companies should define what business they are in, agreeing that the customer must be the starting point of any business. Levitt's emphasis on the importance of defining the business came to be called a functional (function-oriented) definition. One critic defined this as "one enabling a firm's benefit to customers [to be] clearly realized. 'Non-functional,' on the other hand, is a synonym of … 'product-oriented.'"[5]

Today, marketing theory still acknowledges the importance of customer wants and needs. "Marketing Myopia" provided the foundations for many customer–centric marketing strategies. Companies created "augmented products"* by adding extras such as after-sale service that increased the product's value. Companies also tried to make the consumption of a product as memorable as possible for their customers (a practice termed "experiential marketing.")*

Contemporary businesses also need to recognize that giving customers an active role boosts their satisfaction. When consumers engage with the brand, that process increases the value and satisfaction they derive from it. Postmodern marketing* sees the consumer not just as a receiver of the company's products but as an active and equal co-creator of meaning and value; consumers can play an active role by customizing the products or by forming brand communities in which people with an attachment to a particular product can interact.

NOTES

1   John Kay, "Sometimes the Best that a Company can Hope for is Death," The *Financial Times*, August 21, 2013, accessed November 25, 2015, http://www.johnkay.com/2013/08/21/sometimes-the-best-that-a-company-can-hope-for-is-death.

2   Colin Grant, "Theodore Levitt's Marketing Myopia," *Journal of Business Ethics* 18 (1999): 397–406.

3   Theodore Levitt, "HBR Classic: Marketing Myopia," *Harvard Business Review* September–October (1975): 26–8, 33–4, 38–9, 44, 173–4, 176–81.

4   Levitt, "HBR Classic: Marketing Myopia," 181.

5   Koji Wakabayashi, "Relationship Between Business Definition and the Long-term Growth of Companies: Is Levitt Right?" *Pacific Economic Review* 10 (2005): 579.

THE EVOLVING DEBATE

KEY POINTS

- Levitt observed that some businesses have taken a customer orientation* too far by catering to every whim of the customer. He called it "marketing mania."*

- "Marketing Myopia" sparked the development of the functional school of marketing* (the idea of marketing as a decision-making activity that is directed at satisfying customer needs), and the separate discipline of services marketing* (the marketing of services such as hospitality and healthcare rather than products).

- Levitt's ideas remain at the center of academic discussion as thinkers continue to define the qualities necessary for a successful business.

Uses and Problems

Theodore Levitt's "Marketing Myopia" offered a fresh perspective for managers on how to approach their markets and to put their customers at the center of marketing strategies. When it was first published, marketing had not yet developed as an academic discipline. Levitt's views about managers' inability to see what their customers really needed from their products revolutionized thinking in business and academia. One author who examined the contemporary relevance of Levitt's work notes that the article "has been canonized as a marketing classic, a landmark contribution that is regurgitated in countless other articles, case studies and, not least, introductory textbooks."[1]

Critics noted that Levitt did not differentiate between business sectors; he also treated single companies as being representative of an entire industry. He offered customer orientation* as a remedy for a company's slowed or zero growth. But this solution does not apply

> ❝ In short, the organization must learn to think of itself not as producing goods or services, but as *buying customers,* as doing the things that will make people *want* to do business with it. ❞
>
> Theodore Levitt, "Marketing Myopia"

equally to all sectors. Companies producing industrial products benefited more from Levitt's solution than those producing consumer products, who did not need Levitt's prompting to focus on their consumers. In a commentary on "Marketing Myopia" published in 1975, Levitt explained that industrial companies turn out more complex technological products. This "produces salesmen who know the product more than they know the customer ... The result has been a narrow product orientation rather than a liberating customer orientation, and 'service' often suffered."[2]

Levitt further comments that in the wake of "Marketing Myopia," some companies have "become obsessively responsive to every fleeting whim of the customer." He calls this "marketing mania" and reiterates that he intended the article as a "manifesto, not a prescription."[3]

Schools of Thought

"Marketing Myopia" has inspired a number of scholars within the marketing field. Its ideas have formed the basis for many subsequent works. Levitt influenced the development of the functional school of marketing, in which pleasing customers remains essential if companies want to generate profits. The most famous academic whose thinking has been influenced by Levitt's work is the American Philip Kotler,* a widely celebrated professor and business consultant. Kotler's book *Marketing Management,*[4] first published in 1967, is currently in its 14th edition. It has spent many years as part of the core curriculum for business students.

We may trace elements of Theodore Levitt's ideas in Kotler's textbook; Kotler writes, for example, about how organizations must analyze the interests, needs, and wants of the consumers in their markets. This draws on Levitt's concept of customer orientation. Kotler also notes that companies must be more efficient and effective than their competitors. Kotler's rigorous analysis of the concept of customer orientation focuses on how service quality may help companies differentiate themselves in a customer-oriented manner.

With his understanding that pleasing customers is essential if companies are to generate profits, Levitt undoubtedly belongs to the functional school of marketing. But his concept of customer orientation has inspired many approaches outside that community. More specifically, focusing on the service aspects of products has led companies to develop a more service-centered model. This model recognizes services marketing as a separate discipline. And it has also led scholars to advocate that marketing should focus on providing services to consumers.[5] Similarly, the concept of products as goods around which consumers have memorable sensory experiences[6] also has roots in Levitt's concept of customer orientation. The service aspects of products can also be used to satisfy and retain customers.

In Current Scholarship

To assess the importance of "Marketing Myopia" in contemporary marketing, in 2005 English and Irish marketing researchers wrote extended essays on their reactions to Levitt's article: "They [the marketing researchers] are aware that organizations can be extremely shortsighted and that customer orientation is more often honored in the breach than the observance. They have seen myopia for themselves, as it were, and often wonder whether there is an organizational optician in the house …"[7] Similarly, commentators today still reiterate Levitt's customer orientation by advising companies: "Stop chattering about the attributes of the product. Instead, be utterly clear about what it does for those who buy it."[8]

A Japanese scholar, Koji Wakabayashi, recently examined Levitt's "Marketing Myopia" article to "prove … Levitt's hypothesis that a company with the proper definition for its business can survive and grow in spite of fluctuation in the industry to which it belongs."[9] The author examined 50 Japanese firms in the electronics business (including Sony, Canon, Sharp, Pioneer, Casio, and Kyocera) because the environment of this industry changes rapidly in order to keep up with information technology. The findings indicate "there is clearly a positive relationship between functionality of business definition and sales growth rate within a period of six to seven years …"[10]

While Levitt had based his study on only a limited number of unsuccessful companies with improper business definitions, leading to criticism that his advice did not apply universally, this extensive study of one industry bore out his findings.

NOTES

1   Stephen Brown, "Reconsidering the Classics: Reader Response to Marketing Myopia," *Journal of Marketing Management* 21 (2005): 485.

2   Theodore Levitt, "HBR Classic: Marketing Myopia," *Harvard Business Review* September–October (1975): 180.

3   Levitt, "HBR Classic: Marketing Myopia," 180.

4   Philip Kotler, *Marketing Management: Analysis, Planning, and Control* (Englewood Cliffs, NJ: Prentice Hall, 1967).

5   Stephen L. Vargo and Robert F. Lusch, "Evolving to a New Dominant Logic for Marketing," *Journal of Marketing*, 68 (2004): 1–17.

6   Joseph Pine II and James H. Gilmore, *The Experience Economy* (Boston: Harvard Business School Press, 1999).

7   Stephen Brown, "Reconsidering the Classics: Reader Response to 'Marketing Myopia,'" *Journal of Marketing Management* 21 (2005): 478.

8   Don Moyer, "Selling Solutions," *Harvard Business Review* 84 (2006): 192.

9   Koji Wakabayashi, "Relationship Between Business Definition and the Long-term Growth of Companies: Is Levitt Right?" *Pacific Economic Review* 10 (2005): 578.

10 Wakabayashi, "Relationship Between Business Definition," 586.

MODULE 11
IMPACT AND INFLUENCE TODAY

KEY POINTS

- The views Levitt articulated in his article "Marketing Myopia" have been adopted by many companies; scholars still revisit and critique them today.

- When Levitt wrote "Marketing Myopia," companies that defined their business too broadly sometimes diversified, acquiring other businesses that they lacked the skill set to run efficiently.

- Companies should balance a customer orientation with a focus on maintaining a competitive advantage.

Position

Theodore Levitt's "Marketing Myopia" serves as a cautionary tale for top managers. If the business stops growing, that does not mean the market for their product has dried up. It may simply mean that management has focused too narrowly on product and failed to acknowledge consumers' needs and wants: a product orientation* as opposed to a consumer orientation.* Scholars today still discuss Levitt's work and admire his blunt, inspirational, and to-the-point writing style.[1]

Levitt's arguments had an impressively large influence on the business world. The concept of customer orientation applies to a wide range of businesses; so does Levitt's advice that companies should rethink the sectors they are in, looking at it from the customers' perspective. Levitt's ideas now permeate the everyday life of many practitioners, from local business owners to marketing managers of multinational corporations. Business that once focused exclusively on

> ❝ 'Marketing Myopia' was a landmark article, because, for the first time, it made organizations realize that they were in a business of creating value for customers. It created a new mindset for strategists in considering the nature of business. The article created an impetus in thinking in marketing terms. ❞
>
> Sultan Kermally, *Gurus on Marketing*

sales now routinely manage their operations in a customer-oriented manner. Levitt also sparked the development of a new concept— relationship marketing,* a practice founded on the understanding that getting and keeping a customer requires building a relationship.

Interaction

Today, Levitt's advice to define what business a company is really in and his ideas of satisfying the customer has transformed into a focus on "delighting" the customer. "One ice cream company," a commentator noted, "decided they were not in the business of making ice cream but delighting their customers (of all ages) by creating excitement for them."[2] Similarly, an "automotive company believed they were not in the business of making cars but manufacturing comfort and safety." These marketing mindsets developed "because of the influence of gurus like Levitt."[3]

In 2013, the British economist John Kay* noted that not every company has succeeded by redefining its business. For example, oil companies that redefined themselves as being in the energy business diversified into coal in the 1970s and 1980s—but managing coalmines requires different skills than being in the oil industry. As a result, oil companies still make most of their money from oil.[4] Previously, this same scholar criticized Levitt for confusing two economic concepts— the industry and the market. He sees the market as based on consumers' needs while industry remains based on the capabilities of the firm.[5] A company with no skill set in a different area of the same sector (like oil businesses expanding into coal) should not expand its business to that area.

Additionally, Kay criticizes Levitt for making generalizations about different business sectors. When the United States-based retailer JCPenney* decided to remodel its stores, the company hired the same person who designed the retail stores for the Apple computer company. Apple's stores have been hailed as groundbreaking in their use of space, their specific choice of materials, and the way they display the products. But Apple and JCPenney are in very different businesses. Apple sells technology; JCPenney sells clothing and household goods. And the two companies draw customers from different age groups with different income levels. No amount of store remodeling can enable JCPenney to attract Apple's customer base, or generate Apple's profits. The project, Kay notes, did not produce the results the retailer had hoped for.

Some critics argue that Levitt's question, "What business are you in?" remains too vague, easily open to misinterpretation.[6] Some saw Levitt's question as an invitation to diversify. He never intended to suggest this. As critics have noted, diversification can be a recipe for financial disaster when companies merge with or acquire different businesses within the same field.[7]

The Continuing Debate

Although Levitt wrote the article in the latter half of the twentieth century, "Marketing Myopia" still resonates with scholars and management practitioners today. The scholar and business consultant George S. Day,* considered the father of the concept of "market-driven" business, cites both Levitt and the business scholar Peter F. Drucker* as influences. Both writers emphasized that creating and keeping a customer should be central to any business. In an interview

Day offers an example of a company that gets it right:"To me, Amazon is a very market-driven company. They're not just in the business of selling books or CDs ... For most people, dealing with Amazon means having a really pleasurable experience on the Net."[8] But Day cautions that customer focus is not a "one size fits all" activity. Companies need to focus on "identifying the really valuable customers and making superhuman efforts to satisfy them, while devoting lesser effort to less important customers."[9]

Day's comments resonate with critics who caution that focusing solely on customers can ultimately be detrimental.[10] But Levitt had already made that clear when he republished "Marketing Myopia" with additional comments in 1975. Levitt specifically articulated that companies should not cater to their customers too much, calling that behavior "marketing mania."*[11]

NOTES

1   John Quelch, "Bark with Bite," *Financial Times*, January 30, 2012, accessed November 24, 2015, http://www.ft.com/intl/cms/s/2/e8c7db08-4566-11e1–a719–00144feabdc0.html#axzz3sWhUKI8U.

2   Sultan Kermally, "Theodore Levitt," in *Gurus on Marketing* (London: Thorogood, 2003), 47.

3   Sultan Kermally, "Theodore Levitt," 47.

4   John Kay, "Sometimes the Best that a Company can Hope for is Death," The *Financial Times*, August 21, 2013, accessed November 25, 2015, http://www.johnkay.com/2013/08/21/sometimes-the-best-that-a-company-can-hope-for-is-death.

5   John Kay, "Learning to Define the Core Business," The *Financial Times*, December 1, 1995, accessed November 25, 2015, http://www.johnkay.com/1995/12/01/learning-to-define-the-core-business.

6   Donald W. Beard and Gregory G. Dess, "Corporate-Level Strategy, Business-Level Strategy, and Firm Performance," *The Academy of Management Journal* 24 (1981): 663–88.

7   Gerald F. Davis, Kristina A. Diekmann, and Catherine H. Tinsley,
    "The Decline and Fall of the Conglomerate Firm in the 1980s: The
    Deinstitutionalization of an Organizational Form," *American Sociological
    Review* 59 (1994): 547–70.

8   A. J. Vogl, "Getting an Edge," *Across the Board*, February (2000): 47.

9   Vogl, "Getting an Edge," 44.

10 Stephen Brown, "Marketing and Literature: the Anxiety of Academic
    Influence," *Journal of Marketing* 63 (1999): 1–15.

11 Theodore Levitt, "HBR Classic: Marketing Myopia," *Harvard Business Review*
    September–October (1975): 26–8, 33–4, 38–9, 44, 173–4, 176–81.

MODULE 12
WHERE NEXT?

KEY POINTS

- The experience of companies that have benefited tremendously from Levitt's insights can serve as an inspiration for other managers.

- Scholars urge companies to revisit Levitt's ideas to increase the growth of their businesses.

- Levitt's ideas continue to inspire scholars, particularly in Asia. Interest in the applicability of Levitt's views has resurfaced in Japan.

Potential

What kind of an impact has Theodore Levitt's "Marketing Myopia" had on business? Alan G. Lafley,* a former CEO of the US-based consumer products giant Procter & Gamble,* noted that a customer orientation* has been very effective for his company. "By putting customers first, we've nearly doubled the number served, from 2 billion to 3.8 billion; doubled sales; and tripled P&G profits in the first nine years of the twenty-first century."[1] Taking Laffley's advice, companies should continue to focus on their customers.

Recently, scholars have urged management practitioners to pay more attention to Levitt's views on the importance of satisfying the customer: "Most new-product developers don't think in those terms, they've become much too good at creating products that don't help customers do the jobs they need to get done."[2] These authors view the function of advertising as clarifying the nature of the job a product needs to do to satisfy consumers and giving the job (or product) a name that consumers can remember. "To build brands that mean

> **❝ I** began this research project in an attempt to give universal validity to Levitt's hypothesis and to propose prescriptive measures urging businesspeople to carefully define their businesses. **❞**
>
> Koji Wakabayashi, "Relationship Between Business Definition and the Long-term Growth of Companies: Is Levitt Right?"

something to customers, you need to attach them to products that mean something to customers."[3]

Future Directions

"Marketing Myopia" remains an influential article. One commentator noted that Levitt defended "the dignity of marketing" at a time when advertising was seen as immoral because it persuaded people to buy products they did not really need.[4] The distinguished economist John Kenneth Galbraith* and others believed advertising convinced the consumer to consume more. We can see this dynamic playing out in the marketing for luxury high-end brands, not to mention the stereotypical fast-food question "Would you like fries with that?" One may assume that companies producing luxury brands attract wealthy consumers. In reality, affluent customers form just a small segment of the target market for these companies.

One recent article noted that marketing practitioners "still do a surprisingly poor job of marketing," especially in terms of developing trust between sellers and buyers.[5] Applauding Levitt's original article and his notion of customer orientation, the article's authors reiterate that companies should focus on building relationships with their consumers because marketing is more than just selling.[6] Companies should focus on "satisfying customer needs at every income level … by building trust, communicating, and educating consumers, lowering costs, creating choices, and stimulating growth."[7] US brands dominate the global marketplace—eight of the ten most valuable brands in the world are American. Some have credited this, at least in part, to Levitt's work.[8] So in addition to generating continued debates within academia, Levitt's ideas continue to provide useful tools for the business world.

Recently, Asian scholars renewed interest in "Marketing Myopia." In 2005, a Japanese researcher tested the validity of Levitt's argument that a proper business definition sparks growth. The findings suggest that a company that successfully aligns all levels of the business (in their divisions, products, and services) around a functional business definition will experience more growth than its competitors.[9] This confirms Levitt's advice. Future scholars may examine different industries in different markets to see how widely Levitt's theories can apply.

Summary

When Levitt wrote "Marketing Myopia" scholars and businesspeople alike regarded its ideas as revolutionary. The work helped to establish marketing as an academic discipline and Levitt as "the father of modern marketing." Levitt's blunt and pointed analysis of the reasons business growth slowed or stopped appealed to management practitioners. His article also served as a cautionary tale, describing how businesses ran the risk of failing if they did not focus on the wants and needs of their customers.

Levitt specifically wrote his article as a manifesto because he wanted it to serve as a "wake-up call" for businesspeople. By illustrating his arguments with real-world examples, he made it easier for managers to relate to and understand the consequences of a product orientation* as opposed to a customer orientation.

Levitt inspired the functional school of marketing;* subsequent works would increasingly emphasize marketing as a social process. In time, Theodore Levitt's customer orientation developed into a broader market orientation. The postmodern marketing* school took this notion even further, allowing the consumer actively to cocreate products, enhancing their value. The ideas of "Marketing Myopia" have spread across the globe, with many small- and medium-sized enterprises learning Levitt's customer-focused practices, while scholars continue to verify and expand on his ideas. The legacy of "the father of modern marketing" appears to be secure.

NOTES

1   Alan M. Kantrow, "Why Read Peter Drucker?" *Harvard Business Review* 87, November (2009): 73.

2   Clayton M. Christensen et al., "Marketing Malpractice: The Cause and the Cure," *Harvard Business Review* 83 December (2005): 74–83, 152.

3   Christensen et al., "Marketing Malpractice," 82.

4   Aedh Aherne, "Exploit the Levitt Write Cycle," *Journal of Strategic Marketing* 14 March (2006): 79.

5   John A. Quelch and Katherine E. Jocz, "For the Greater Goods," *The American: A Magazine of Ideas*, November–December (2008): 77.

6   Quelch and Jocz, "For the Greater Goods," 77.

7   Quelch and Jocz, "For the Greater Goods," 73–4.

8   Quelch and Jocz, "For the Greater Goods," 73–4.

9   Koji Wakabayashi, "Relationship between Business Definition and Corporate Growth: The Effect of Functional Alignment," *Pacific Economic Review* 13 (2008): 663–79.

GLOSSARY

GLOSSARY OF TERMS

Antioch College: a progressive American university located in Yellow Springs, Ohio.

Apple: a company that specializes in technology products such as computers and smart phones. Other notable products include the iPad, the iPod and the Apple watch.

Augmented product: nonphysical attributes such as after-sale service added to a physical product to increase the product's value.

Baby boom generation: people born between 1946 and 1964. The optimism associated with the end of World War II led to an increase in the birth rate in the United States. The baby boom generation is the largest cohort of people the United States has ever seen.

Brand communities: voluntary communities of consumers formed on the basis of attachment to a particular product. An example is the online brand community My Starbucks Idea, associated with the coffee shop chain Starbucks. As a result of suggestions in this community, Starbucks has introduced cup recycling and coconut milk as a nondairy milk option in some stores; it has also indicated a commitment to hire military veterans and their spouses.

Conspicuous consumption: a term coined by the American economist Thorstein Veblen, whose most famous book is *The Theory of the Leisure Class* (1899). It means spending money on (luxury) goods to impress others and display one's social status. Examples might include purchasing a Rolex watch or a designer handbag—or even a counterfeit of these items—if the intent is to impress someone else rather than to just tell the time or carry one's belongings.

Customer orientation: the prioritization of consumer needs as the starting point and main drive behind a company's business activities. Companies with a customer orientation primarily concern themselves with satisfying consumers.

DuPont: a large industrial and global enterprise, founded in the United States in 1802. Originally focused on producing gunpowder and dynamite, DuPont started producing synthetic fibers including nylon in 1935. Today, DuPont produces a wide range of products: biotechnology including biofuels (cellulosic ethanol), agricultural products (seeds and crop protection), food (proteins, enzymes, and additives), plastic, construction materials, cosmetics, and packaging materials.

Economies of scale: the cost advantages that arise with increased output of a product. The greater the quantity of goods produced, the lower the cost per unit because the fixed production costs are shared over a larger number of products.

Experiential marketing: a strategy focusing on the sensory experience that a product or service can provide to the customer. The goal is to create a closer bond between the consumers and the brand by making the process of consuming the product as memorable as possible.

Functional school of marketing: the view of marketing as a decision-making activity directed at satisfying customer needs, understanding that pleasing customers remains essential for companies to generate profits.

General Motors: a multinational automotive company headquartered in Detroit, Michigan. Its car and truck brands include Buick, Cadillac, Chevrolet, GMC, Opel, and Vauxhall.

Globalization of markets: as markets around the world become linked by technology, consumers' needs become homogenized. Similar, standardized consumer products appear in markets around the world as more efficient transportation and distribution options make overseas markets accessible to companies everywhere.

Harvard Business Review: a prestigious management magazine, founded in 1922 and published 10 times a year by Harvard University subsidiary Harvard Business Publishing.

Harvard Business School: a prestigious graduate business school and part of Harvard University in Cambridge, Massachusetts.

JCPenney: a retailer in the United States with more than 1,000 stores nationwide. The company primarily sells clothes, beauty products, and household items

Marketing mania: a term coined by Theodore Levitt. It means that companies can cater too much to the needs and wants of their customers.

Marketing matrix: a visual tool that measures how well a company meets customers' key requirements in terms of product, price, place, and promotion.

Marketing mix classification: a concept popularized by Philip Kotler in his book *Marketing Management* (1967). It is considered an essential tool in marketing and involves the 4 P's: product, price, place, and promotion.

Nazi Party: political party, founded in 1919, that gained power in Germany under Adolf Hitler's leadership. The Nazi Party, which advocated German pride and promoted anti-Semitism, ruled

Germany from 1933 to 1945. After Germany's defeat in World War II (1939–45), the Nazi Party was outlawed and many of its officials were convicted of war crimes.

Ohio State University: an educational establishment established in 1870 and located in Columbus, Ohio. With 570 buildings on a main campus of 1,900 acres and more than 58,000 students, Ohio State is the largest university in the United States.

Postmodern marketing: a marketing movement influenced by a critical philosophical stance that prioritizes individualistic demands and differences and rejects broad market generalizations. Customers are collaborators—they design the products tailored to their own unique and individual preferences.

Postmodern world: the era following modernity. Generally accepted as beginning in the late twentieth century.

Procter & Gamble: a US-based company, manufacturer of consumer goods, household cleaning products, and personal care products.

Product customization: the opportunity for consumers to individualize the product they are buying to suit their unique preferences.

Product orientation: a business philosophy in which a company's main product drives its business activities and management decisions.

Relationship marketing: a strategy designed to increase customer loyalty by building a long-term relationship, with a focus on retaining customers as opposed to acquiring new ones.

Research and development (R&D): work aimed at developing new (industrial) methods, materials, products, and knowledge. Most large businesses have a research and development department.

Services marketing: the marketing of services rather than products. Examples include financial services, hospitality, and healthcare.

Standard Oil: an oil company, once the largest oil company in the United States; its successor companies are Exxon Mobil, Chevron, BP, and Marathon.

Strategic marketing: marketing approach that involves identifying a company's competitive advantage in its intended market. The next step would be to use the company's marketing resources to increase sales of its product in that market.

University of North Dakota: North Dakota's oldest and largest university. The university, located in Grand Forks, ND, has nearly 15,000 students.

Value-in-use: the benefits customers enjoy by consuming a particular product or service. These may be utilitarian or symbolic benefits. For example, using a product to display one's status gives value to the consumer.

World War II: global conflict that took place between 1939 and 1945, first on European soil and later also in the Pacific. The United States became involved in 1941 after the Japanese bombed Pearl Harbor in Hawaii. The war officially ended when Japan surrendered on August 14, 1945.

PEOPLE MENTIONED IN THE TEXT

Wroe Alderson (1898–1965) was a marketing theorist and founder of the marketing consulting firm Alderson Associates. He taught at the University of Pennsylvania (The Wharton School). Alderson applied mathematical models to build a scientific basis for marketing research. He is best known for his book *Marketing Behavior and Executive Action* (1957).

Neil H. Borden (1895–1980) was a professor at Harvard Business School for more than 40 years. He also served as president of the American Marketing Association. Borden wrote *The Concept of the Marketing Mix* (1964), in which he outlined the different elements in marketing products to consumers. He is primarily remembered for his impact on the understanding and practice of advertising management.

George S. Day (b. 1937) is a Canadian-born professor emeritus of marketing and former director of the Huntsman Center for Global Competition and Innovation at the University of Pennsylvania's Wharton School (1991–2000). He also consults with corporations such as AT&T and General Electric. His most recent book is *Innovation Prowess: Leadership Strategies for Accelerating Growth* (2013).

Peter F. Drucker (1909–2005) was a distinguished academic in the field of management and a business consultant working for companies including General Motors, IBM, and General Electric. He wrote more than 30 books. His publication *The Practice of Management* (1954) has been voted the third most influential book of the twentieth century. In 2002 he received the Presidential Medal of Freedom, the highest civilian honor in the United States.

John Kenneth Galbraith (1908–2006) was a Canadian-born American economist who was a professor at Harvard University. His 1958 book *The Affluent Society* became a best seller and made him well known around the world. In 1960, President John F. Kennedy appointed him the United States ambassador to India. He later served as adviser to Kennedy's successor, Lyndon B. Johnson. He wrote many best selling books and in 2000 President Bill Clinton awarded him the Medal of Freedom, the highest civilian honor in the United States.

Adolf Hitler (1889–1945) was an Austrian-born politician whose Nazi Party gained power in Germany in 1933. His invasion of Poland started World War II. He also orchestrated the Holocaust, during which more than six million Jewish people, homosexuals, and other "undesirables" were murdered.

John Kay (b. 1948) is a Scottish-born economist and former chair of the London Business School, who established a consultancy business called London Economics. He has written many books including *The Business of Economics* (1996), *Culture and Prosperity: The Truth About Markets – Why Some Nations are Rich but Most Remain Poor* (2004), and *Other People's Money* (2015). Since 1995, he has written a weekly column for the *Financial Times*, a London-based newspaper.

Philip Kotler (b. 1931) is S. C. Johnson & Son Distinguished Professor of International Marketing at the Kellogg School of Management at Northwestern University in Evanston, Illinois. He has written more than 40 influential books in the field of marketing, establishing himself as a guru in the discipline. His book *Marketing Management: Analysis, Planning, and Control* (first published in 1967 and now in its 14th edition) remains core reading for business students.

Alan G. Lafley (b. 1947) is an American businessman. He served as CEO (chief executive officer) of Procter & Gamble from 2000 to 2009 and again from 2013 to 2015. Lafley focused on consumer-driven innovation. He received his MBA from Harvard Business School.

Thorstein Veblen (1857–1929) was an American economist, and is well known for articulating the concept of "conspicuous consumption." He taught at the University of Chicago, Stanford University, and the University of Missouri. Veblen wrote many books, including *The Theory of the Leisure Class* (1899), *The Theory of Business Enterprise* (1904), and *The Engineers and the Price System* (1921).

WORKS CITED

WORKS CITED

Aherne, Aedh. "Exploit the Levitt Write Cycle." *Journal of Strategic Marketing* 14 (2006): 77–87.

Alderson, Wroe. *Marketing Behavior and Executive Action: A Functionalist Approach to Marketing Theory*. Homewood, IL: Richard D. Irwin, 1957.

Bailey, Jan. "Profile on Theodore Levitt: the Father of Modern Marketing." *Engineering Management* 16 (2006): 48–9.

Beard, Donald W. and Gregory G. Dess. "Corporate-Level Strategy, Business-Level Strategy, and Firm Performance." *The Academy of Management Journal* 24 (1981): 663–88.

Brown, Stephen. "Marketing and Literature: the Anxiety of Academic Influence." *Journal of Marketing* 63 (1999): 1–15.

"Reconsidering the Classics: Reader Response to 'Marketing Myopia.'" *Journal of Marketing Management* 21 (2005): 473–87.

Christensen, Clayton M., Scott Cook, and Taddy Hall. "Marketing Malpractice: The Cause and the Cure." *Harvard Business Review* 83 (2005): 74–83, 152.

Davis, Gerald F., Kristina A. Diekmann, and Catherine H. Tinsley. "The Decline and Fall of the Conglomerate Firm in the 1980s: The Deinstitutionalization of an Organizational Form." *American Sociological Review* 59 (1994): 547–70.

Drucker, Peter F. *Concept of the Corporation*. New York: Day, 1946.

Managing for Results. New York: Harper & Row, 1964.

The Practice of Management. New York: Harper & Row, 1954.

Feder, Barnaby J. "Theodore Levitt, 81, Who Coined the Term 'Globalization,' Is Dead." The *New York Times*, July 6, 2006. Accessed November 7, 2015. www.nytimes.com/2006/07/06/business/06levitt.html.

Galbraith, John Kenneth. *The Affluent Society*. Boston, Mass.: Houghton Mifflin, 1958.

Grant, Colin. "Theodore Levitt's Marketing Myopia." *Journal of Business Ethics* 18 (1999): 397–406.

Harvard University Gazette. "Professor Theodore Levitt, Legendary Marketing Scholar and Former Harvard Business Review Editor, Dead at 81." *Harvard University Gazette*, July 20, 2006. Accessed November 7, 2015. http://news.harvard.edu/gazette/2006/07.20/99–levitt.html.

Kantrow, Alan M. "Why Read Peter Drucker?" *Harvard Business Review* 87, November (2009): 72–82.

Kay, John. "Learning to Define the Core Business." The *Financial Times*, December 01, 1995. Accessed November 25, 2015. http://www.johnkay. com/1995/12/01/learning-to-define-the-core-business.

"Sometimes the Best that a Company can Hope for is Death." The *Financial Times*, August 21, 2013. Accessed November 25, 2015. http://www.johnkay. com/2013/08/21/sometimes-the-best-that-a-company-can-hope-for-is-death.

Kermally, Sultan. "Theodore Levitt." In *Gurus on Marketing*, 43–56. London: Thorogood, 2003.

Kotler, Philip. *Marketing Management: Analysis, Planning, and Control*. Englewood Cliffs, NJ: Prentice-Hall, 1967.

Levitt, Theodore. "The Globalization of Markets." *Harvard Business Review* May/June (1983): 92–102.

"HBR Classic: Marketing Myopia." *Harvard Business Review* September–October (1975): 26–8, 33–4, 38–9, 44, 173–4, 176–81.

Marketing for Business Growth. New York: McGraw-Hill, 1974.

The Marketing Imagination. New York: Free Press, 1983.

"Marketing Myopia." *Harvard Business Review* July–August (1960): 45–56.

Thinking About Management. New York: Free Press, 1991.

Moyer, Don. "Selling Solutions." *Harvard Business Review* 84 (July–August 2006): 192.

O'Brien, Jeffrey M. "Drums in the Jungle." *MC: Technology Marketing Intelligence* 19 (1999): 22–6.

Ottman, Jacquelyn and Mark Eisen. "Green Marketing Myopia and the SunChips Snacklash." *Harvard Business Review Blog Network* (2010). Accessed December 7, 2013. http://blogs.hbr.org/2010/10/green-marketing-myopia-and-the/

Pine, Joseph II and James H. Gilmore. *The Experience Economy*. Boston: Harvard Business School Press, 1999.

Quelch, John. "Bark with Bite." The *Financial Times*, January 30, 2012. Accessed November 25, 2015. http://www.ft.com/intl/cms/s/2/e8c7db08-4566-11e1–a719–00144feabdc0.html#axzz3sWhUKI8U.

Quelch, John and Katherine E. Jocz, "For the Greater Goods." *The American: A Magazine of Ideas*, November–December (2008): 72–7.

Spaulding, Elizabeth and Christopher Perry. "Making it Personal: Rules for Success in Product Customization." *Bain Insights Newsletter*, September 16, 2013. Accessed November 23, 2015. http://www.bain.com/publications/articles/making-it-personal-rules-for-success-in-product-customization.aspx.

Vargo, Stephen L. and Robert F. Lusch. "Evolving to a New Dominant Logic for Marketing." *Journal of Marketing* 68 (2004): 1–17.

Veblen, Thorstein. *The Theory of the Leisure Class*. Auckland: Floating Press, 1899.

Vogl, A. J. "Getting an Edge." *Across the Board*, February (2000): 43–8.

Vohra, Neharika and Kumar Mukul. "Relevance of Peter Drucker's Work: Celebrating Drucker's 100th Birthday." *Vikalpa* 34 (2009): 1–7.

Wakabayashi, Koji. "Relationship between Business Definition and Corporate Growth: The Effect of Functional Alignment." *Pacific Economic Review* 13 (2008): 663–79.

"Relationship between Business Definition and the Long-Term Growth of Companies: Is Levitt Right?" *Pacific Economic Review* 10 (2005): 577–89.

THE MACAT LIBRARY
BY DISCIPLINE

AFRICANA STUDIES

Chinua Achebe's *An Image of Africa: Racism in Conrad's Heart of Darkness*
W. E. B. Du Bois's *The Souls of Black Folk*
Zora Neale Huston's *Characteristics of Negro Expression*
Martin Luther King Jr's *Why We Can't Wait*
Toni Morrison's *Playing in the Dark: Whiteness in the American Literary Imagination*

ANTHROPOLOGY

Arjun Appadurai's *Modernity at Large: Cultural Dimensions of Globalisation*
Philippe Ariès's *Centuries of Childhood*
Franz Boas's *Race, Language and Culture*
Kim Chan & Renée Mauborgne's *Blue Ocean Strategy*
Jared Diamond's *Guns, Germs & Steel: the Fate of Human Societies*
Jared Diamond's *Collapse: How Societies Choose to Fail or Survive*
E. E. Evans-Pritchard's *Witchcraft, Oracles and Magic Among the Azande*
James Ferguson's *The Anti-Politics Machine*
Clifford Geertz's *The Interpretation of Cultures*
David Graeber's *Debt: the First 5000 Years*
Karen Ho's *Liquidated: An Ethnography of Wall Street*
Geert Hofstede's *Culture's Consequences: Comparing Values, Behaviors, Institutes and Organizations across Nations*
Claude Lévi-Strauss's *Structural Anthropology*
Jay Macleod's *Ain't No Makin' It: Aspirations and Attainment in a Low-Income Neighborhood*
Saba Mahmood's *The Politics of Piety: The Islamic Revival and the Feminist Subject*
Marcel Mauss's *The Gift*

BUSINESS

Jean Lave & Etienne Wenger's *Situated Learning*
Theodore Levitt's *Marketing Myopia*
Burton G. Malkiel's *A Random Walk Down Wall Street*
Douglas McGregor's *The Human Side of Enterprise*
Michael Porter's *Competitive Strategy: Creating and Sustaining Superior Performance*
John Kotter's *Leading Change*
C. K. Prahalad & Gary Hamel's *The Core Competence of the Corporation*

CRIMINOLOGY

Michelle Alexander's *The New Jim Crow: Mass Incarceration in the Age of Colorblindness*
Michael R. Gottfredson & Travis Hirschi's *A General Theory of Crime*
Richard Herrnstein & Charles A. Murray's *The Bell Curve: Intelligence and Class Structure in American Life*
Elizabeth Loftus's *Eyewitness Testimony*
Jay Macleod's *Ain't No Makin' It: Aspirations and Attainment in a Low-Income Neighborhood*
Philip Zimbardo's *The Lucifer Effect*

ECONOMICS

Janet Abu-Lughod's *Before European Hegemony*
Ha-Joon Chang's *Kicking Away the Ladder*
David Brion Davis's *The Problem of Slavery in the Age of Revolution*
Milton Friedman's *The Role of Monetary Policy*
Milton Friedman's *Capitalism and Freedom*
David Graeber's *Debt: the First 5000 Years*
Friedrich Hayek's *The Road to Serfdom*
Karen Ho's *Liquidated: An Ethnography of Wall Street*

John Maynard Keynes's *The General Theory of Employment, Interest and Money*
Charles P. Kindleberger's *Manias, Panics and Crashes*
Robert Lucas's *Why Doesn't Capital Flow from Rich to Poor Countries?*
Burton G. Malkiel's *A Random Walk Down Wall Street*
Thomas Robert Malthus's *An Essay on the Principle of Population*
Karl Marx's *Capital*
Thomas Piketty's *Capital in the Twenty-First Century*
Amartya Sen's *Development as Freedom*
Adam Smith's *The Wealth of Nations*
Nassim Nicholas Taleb's *The Black Swan: The Impact of the Highly Improbable*
Amos Tversky's & Daniel Kahneman's *Judgment under Uncertainty: Heuristics and Biases*
Mahbub Ul Haq's *Reflections on Human Development*
Max Weber's *The Protestant Ethic and the Spirit of Capitalism*

FEMINISM AND GENDER STUDIES

Judith Butler's *Gender Trouble*
Simone De Beauvoir's *The Second Sex*
Michel Foucault's *History of Sexuality*
Betty Friedan's *The Feminine Mystique*
Saba Mahmood's *The Politics of Piety: The Islamic Revival and the Feminist Subject*
Joan Wallach Scott's *Gender and the Politics of History*
Mary Wollstonecraft's *A Vindication of the Rights of Woman*
Virginia Woolf's *A Room of One's Own*

GEOGRAPHY

The Brundtland Report's *Our Common Future*
Rachel Carson's *Silent Spring*
Charles Darwin's *On the Origin of Species*
James Ferguson's *The Anti-Politics Machine*
Jane Jacobs's *The Death and Life of Great American Cities*
James Lovelock's *Gaia: A New Look at Life on Earth*
Amartya Sen's *Development as Freedom*
Mathis Wackernagel & William Rees's *Our Ecological Footprint*

HISTORY

Janet Abu-Lughod's *Before European Hegemony*
Benedict Anderson's *Imagined Communities*
Bernard Bailyn's *The Ideological Origins of the American Revolution*
Hanna Batatu's *The Old Social Classes And The Revolutionary Movements Of Iraq*
Christopher Browning's *Ordinary Men: Reserve Police Batallion 101 and the Final Solution in Poland*
Edmund Burke's *Reflections on the Revolution in France*
William Cronon's *Nature's Metropolis: Chicago And The Great West*
Alfred W. Crosby's *The Columbian Exchange*
Hamid Dabashi's *Iran: A People Interrupted*
David Brion Davis's *The Problem of Slavery in the Age of Revolution*
Nathalie Zemon Davis's *The Return of Martin Guerre*
Jared Diamond's *Guns, Germs & Steel: the Fate of Human Societies*
Frank Dikotter's *Mao's Great Famine*
John W Dower's *War Without Mercy: Race And Power In The Pacific War*
W. E. B. Du Bois's *The Souls of Black Folk*
Richard J. Evans's *In Defence of History*
Lucien Febvre's *The Problem of Unbelief in the 16th Century*
Sheila Fitzpatrick's *Everyday Stalinism*

The Macat Library By Discipline

Eric Foner's *Reconstruction: America's Unfinished Revolution, 1863-1877*
Michel Foucault's *Discipline and Punish*
Michel Foucault's *History of Sexuality*
Francis Fukuyama's *The End of History and the Last Man*
John Lewis Gaddis's *We Now Know: Rethinking Cold War History*
Ernest Gellner's *Nations and Nationalism*
Eugene Genovese's *Roll, Jordan, Roll: The World the Slaves Made*
Carlo Ginzburg's *The Night Battles*
Daniel Goldhagen's *Hitler's Willing Executioners*
Jack Goldstone's *Revolution and Rebellion in the Early Modern World*
Antonio Gramsci's *The Prison Notebooks*
Alexander Hamilton, John Jay & James Madison's *The Federalist Papers*
Christopher Hill's *The World Turned Upside Down*
Carole Hillenbrand's *The Crusades: Islamic Perspectives*
Thomas Hobbes's *Leviathan*
Eric Hobsbawm's *The Age Of Revolution*
John A. Hobson's *Imperialism: A Study*
Albert Hourani's *History of the Arab Peoples*
Samuel P. Huntington's *The Clash of Civilizations and the Remaking of World Order*
C. L. R. James's *The Black Jacobins*
Tony Judt's *Postwar: A History of Europe Since 1945*
Ernst Kantorowicz's *The King's Two Bodies: A Study in Medieval Political Theology*
Paul Kennedy's *The Rise and Fall of the Great Powers*
Ian Kershaw's *The "Hitler Myth": Image and Reality in the Third Reich*
John Maynard Keynes's *The General Theory of Employment, Interest and Money*
Charles P. Kindleberger's *Manias, Panics and Crashes*
Martin Luther King Jr's *Why We Can't Wait*
Henry Kissinger's *World Order: Reflections on the Character of Nations and the Course of History*
Thomas Kuhn's *The Structure of Scientific Revolutions*
Georges Lefebvre's *The Coming of the French Revolution*
John Locke's *Two Treatises of Government*
Niccolò Machiavelli's *The Prince*
Thomas Robert Malthus's *An Essay on the Principle of Population*
Mahmood Mamdani's *Citizen and Subject: Contemporary Africa And The Legacy Of Late Colonialism*
Karl Marx's *Capital*
Stanley Milgram's *Obedience to Authority*
John Stuart Mill's *On Liberty*
Thomas Paine's *Common Sense*
Thomas Paine's *Rights of Man*
Geoffrey Parker's *Global Crisis: War, Climate Change and Catastrophe in the Seventeenth Century*
Jonathan Riley-Smith's *The First Crusade and the Idea of Crusading*
Jean-Jacques Rousseau's *The Social Contract*
Joan Wallach Scott's *Gender and the Politics of History*
Theda Skocpol's *States and Social Revolutions*
Adam Smith's *The Wealth of Nations*
Timothy Snyder's *Bloodlands: Europe Between Hitler and Stalin*
Sun Tzu's *The Art of War*
Keith Thomas's *Religion and the Decline of Magic*
Thucydides's *The History of the Peloponnesian War*
Frederick Jackson Turner's *The Significance of the Frontier in American History*
Odd Arne Westad's *The Global Cold War: Third World Interventions And The Making Of Our Times*

LITERATURE

Chinua Achebe's *An Image of Africa: Racism in Conrad's Heart of Darkness*
Roland Barthes's *Mythologies*
Homi K. Bhabha's *The Location of Culture*
Judith Butler's *Gender Trouble*
Simone De Beauvoir's *The Second Sex*
Ferdinand De Saussure's *Course in General Linguistics*
T. S. Eliot's *The Sacred Wood: Essays on Poetry and Criticism*
Zora Neale Huston's *Characteristics of Negro Expression*
Toni Morrison's *Playing in the Dark: Whiteness in the American Literary Imagination*
Edward Said's *Orientalism*
Gayatri Chakravorty Spivak's *Can the Subaltern Speak?*
Mary Wollstonecraft's *A Vindication of the Rights of Women*
Virginia Woolf's *A Room of One's Own*

PHILOSOPHY

Elizabeth Anscombe's *Modern Moral Philosophy*
Hannah Arendt's *The Human Condition*
Aristotle's *Metaphysics*
Aristotle's *Nicomachean Ethics*
Edmund Gettier's *Is Justified True Belief Knowledge?*
Georg Wilhelm Friedrich Hegel's *Phenomenology of Spirit*
David Hume's *Dialogues Concerning Natural Religion*
David Hume's *The Enquiry for Human Understanding*
Immanuel Kant's *Religion within the Boundaries of Mere Reason*
Immanuel Kant's *Critique of Pure Reason*
Søren Kierkegaard's *The Sickness Unto Death*
Søren Kierkegaard's *Fear and Trembling*
C. S. Lewis's *The Abolition of Man*
Alasdair MacIntyre's *After Virtue*
Marcus Aurelius's *Meditations*
Friedrich Nietzsche's *On the Genealogy of Morality*
Friedrich Nietzsche's *Beyond Good and Evil*
Plato's *Republic*
Plato's *Symposium*
Jean-Jacques Rousseau's *The Social Contract*
Gilbert Ryle's *The Concept of Mind*
Baruch Spinoza's *Ethics*
Sun Tzu's *The Art of War*
Ludwig Wittgenstein's *Philosophical Investigations*

POLITICS

Benedict Anderson's *Imagined Communities*
Aristotle's *Politics*
Bernard Bailyn's *The Ideological Origins of the American Revolution*
Edmund Burke's *Reflections on the Revolution in France*
John C. Calhoun's *A Disquisition on Government*
Ha-Joon Chang's *Kicking Away the Ladder*
Hamid Dabashi's *Iran: A People Interrupted*
Hamid Dabashi's *Theology of Discontent: The Ideological Foundation of the Islamic Revolution in Iran*
Robert Dahl's *Democracy and its Critics*
Robert Dahl's *Who Governs?*
David Brion Davis's *The Problem of Slavery in the Age of Revolution*

The Macat Library By Discipline

Alexis De Tocqueville's *Democracy in America*
James Ferguson's *The Anti-Politics Machine*
Frank Dikotter's *Mao's Great Famine*
Sheila Fitzpatrick's *Everyday Stalinism*
Eric Foner's *Reconstruction: America's Unfinished Revolution, 1863-1877*
Milton Friedman's *Capitalism and Freedom*
Francis Fukuyama's *The End of History and the Last Man*
John Lewis Gaddis's *We Now Know: Rethinking Cold War History*
Ernest Gellner's *Nations and Nationalism*
David Graeber's *Debt: the First 5000 Years*
Antonio Gramsci's *The Prison Notebooks*
Alexander Hamilton, John Jay & James Madison's *The Federalist Papers*
Friedrich Hayek's *The Road to Serfdom*
Christopher Hill's *The World Turned Upside Down*
Thomas Hobbes's *Leviathan*
John A. Hobson's *Imperialism: A Study*
Samuel P. Huntington's *The Clash of Civilizations and the Remaking of World Order*
Tony Judt's *Postwar: A History of Europe Since 1945*
David C. Kang's *China Rising: Peace, Power and Order in East Asia*
Paul Kennedy's *The Rise and Fall of Great Powers*
Robert Keohane's *After Hegemony*
Martin Luther King Jr.'s *Why We Can't Wait*
Henry Kissinger's *World Order: Reflections on the Character of Nations and the Course of History*
John Locke's *Two Treatises of Government*
Niccolò Machiavelli's *The Prince*
Thomas Robert Malthus's *An Essay on the Principle of Population*
Mahmood Mamdani's *Citizen and Subject: Contemporary Africa And The Legacy Of Late Colonialism*
Karl Marx's *Capital*
John Stuart Mill's *On Liberty*
John Stuart Mill's *Utilitarianism*
Hans Morgenthau's *Politics Among Nations*
Thomas Paine's *Common Sense*
Thomas Paine's *Rights of Man*
Thomas Piketty's *Capital in the Twenty-First Century*
Robert D. Putman's *Bowling Alone*
John Rawls's *Theory of Justice*
Jean-Jacques Rousseau's *The Social Contract*
Theda Skocpol's *States and Social Revolutions*
Adam Smith's *The Wealth of Nations*
Sun Tzu's *The Art of War*
Henry David Thoreau's *Civil Disobedience*
Thucydides's *The History of the Peloponnesian War*
Kenneth Waltz's *Theory of International Politics*
Max Weber's *Politics as a Vocation*
Odd Arne Westad's *The Global Cold War: Third World Interventions And The Making Of Our Times*

POSTCOLONIAL STUDIES

Roland Barthes's *Mythologies*
Frantz Fanon's *Black Skin, White Masks*
Homi K. Bhabha's *The Location of Culture*
Gustavo Gutiérrez's *A Theology of Liberation*
Edward Said's *Orientalism*
Gayatri Chakravorty Spivak's *Can the Subaltern Speak?*

PSYCHOLOGY

Gordon Allport's *The Nature of Prejudice*
Alan Baddeley & Graham Hitch's *Aggression: A Social Learning Analysis*
Albert Bandura's *Aggression: A Social Learning Analysis*
Leon Festinger's *A Theory of Cognitive Dissonance*
Sigmund Freud's *The Interpretation of Dreams*
Betty Friedan's *The Feminine Mystique*
Michael R. Gottfredson & Travis Hirschi's *A General Theory of Crime*
Eric Hoffer's *The True Believer: Thoughts on the Nature of Mass Movements*
William James's *Principles of Psychology*
Elizabeth Loftus's *Eyewitness Testimony*
A. H. Maslow's *A Theory of Human Motivation*
Stanley Milgram's *Obedience to Authority*
Steven Pinker's *The Better Angels of Our Nature*
Oliver Sacks's *The Man Who Mistook His Wife For a Hat*
Richard Thaler & Cass Sunstein's *Nudge: Improving Decisions About Health, Wealth and Happiness*
Amos Tversky's *Judgment under Uncertainty: Heuristics and Biases*
Philip Zimbardo's *The Lucifer Effect*

SCIENCE

Rachel Carson's *Silent Spring*
William Cronon's *Nature's Metropolis: Chicago And The Great West*
Alfred W. Crosby's *The Columbian Exchange*
Charles Darwin's *On the Origin of Species*
Richard Dawkin's *The Selfish Gene*
Thomas Kuhn's *The Structure of Scientific Revolutions*
Geoffrey Parker's *Global Crisis: War, Climate Change and Catastrophe in the Seventeenth Century*
Mathis Wackernagel & William Rees's *Our Ecological Footprint*

SOCIOLOGY

Michelle Alexander's *The New Jim Crow: Mass Incarceration in the Age of Colorblindness*
Gordon Allport's *The Nature of Prejudice*
Albert Bandura's *Aggression: A Social Learning Analysis*
Hanna Batatu's *The Old Social Classes And The Revolutionary Movements Of Iraq*
Ha-Joon Chang's *Kicking Away the Ladder*
W. E. B. Du Bois's *The Souls of Black Folk*
Émile Durkheim's *On Suicide*
Frantz Fanon's *Black Skin, White Masks*
Frantz Fanon's *The Wretched of the Earth*
Eric Foner's *Reconstruction: America's Unfinished Revolution, 1863-1877*
Eugene Genovese's *Roll, Jordan, Roll: The World the Slaves Made*
Jack Goldstone's *Revolution and Rebellion in the Early Modern World*
Antonio Gramsci's *The Prison Notebooks*
Richard Herrnstein & Charles A Murray's *The Bell Curve: Intelligence and Class Structure in American Life*
Eric Hoffer's *The True Believer: Thoughts on the Nature of Mass Movements*
Jane Jacobs's *The Death and Life of Great American Cities*
Robert Lucas's *Why Doesn't Capital Flow from Rich to Poor Countries?*
Jay Macleod's *Ain't No Makin' It: Aspirations and Attainment in a Low Income Neighborhood*
Elaine May's *Homeward Bound: American Families in the Cold War Era*
Douglas McGregor's *The Human Side of Enterprise*
C. Wright Mills's *The Sociological Imagination*

Thomas Piketty's *Capital in the Twenty-First Century*
Robert D. Putman's *Bowling Alone*
David Riesman's *The Lonely Crowd: A Study of the Changing American Character*
Edward Said's *Orientalism*
Joan Wallach Scott's *Gender and the Politics of History*
Theda Skocpol's *States and Social Revolutions*
Max Weber's *The Protestant Ethic and the Spirit of Capitalism*

THEOLOGY

Augustine's *Confessions*
Benedict's *Rule of St Benedict*
Gustavo Gutiérrez's *A Theology of Liberation*
Carole Hillenbrand's *The Crusades: Islamic Perspectives*
David Hume's *Dialogues Concerning Natural Religion*
Immanuel Kant's *Religion within the Boundaries of Mere Reason*
Ernst Kantorowicz's *The King's Two Bodies: A Study in Medieval Political Theology*
Søren Kierkegaard's *The Sickness Unto Death*
C. S. Lewis's *The Abolition of Man*
Saba Mahmood's *The Politics of Piety: The Islamic Revival and the Feminist Subjec*t
Baruch Spinoza's *Ethics*
Keith Thomas's *Religion and the Decline of Magic*

COMING SOON

Chris Argyris's *The Individual and the Organisation*
Seyla Benhabib's *The Rights of Others*
Walter Benjamin's *The Work Of Art in the Age of Mechanical Reproduction*
John Berger's *Ways of Seeing*
Pierre Bourdieu's *Outline of a Theory of Practice*
Mary Douglas's *Purity and Danger*
Roland Dworkin's *Taking Rights Seriously*
James G. March's *Exploration and Exploitation in Organisational Learning*
Ikujiro Nonaka's *A Dynamic Theory of Organizational Knowledge Creation*
Griselda Pollock's *Vision and Difference*
Amartya Sen's *Inequality Re-Examined*
Susan Sontag's *On Photography*
Yasser Tabbaa's *The Transformation of Islamic Art*
Ludwig von Mises's *Theory of Money and Credit*

Macat Disciplines

Access the greatest ideas and thinkers across entire disciplines, including

MAN AND THE ENVIRONMENT

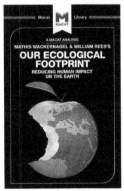

The Brundtland Report's, *Our Common Future*
Rachel Carson's, *Silent Spring*
James Lovelock's, *Gaia: A New Look at Life on Earth*
Mathis Wackernagel & William Rees's, *Our Ecological Footprint*

Macat analyses are available from all good bookshops and libraries.

Access hundreds of analyses through one, multimedia tool.
Join free for one month **library.macat.com**

Macat Pairs

Analyse historical and modern issues from opposite sides of an argument. Pairs include:

ARE WE FUNDAMENTALLY GOOD - OR BAD?

Steven Pinker's
The Better Angels of Our Nature

Stephen Pinker's gloriously optimistic 2011 book argues that, despite humanity's biological tendency toward violence, we are, in fact, less violent today than ever before. To prove his case, Pinker lays out pages of detailed statistical evidence. For him, much of the credit for the decline goes to the eighteenth-century Enlightenment movement, whose ideas of liberty, tolerance, and respect for the value of human life filtered down through society and affected how people thought. That psychological change led to behavioral change—and overall we became more peaceful. Critics countered that humanity could never overcome the biological urge toward violence; others argued that Pinker's statistics were flawed.

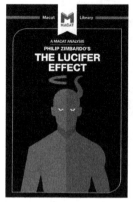

Philip Zimbardo's
The Lucifer Effect

Some psychologists believe those who commit cruelty are innately evil. Zimbardo disagrees. In *The Lucifer Effect*, he argues that sometimes good people do evil things simply because of the situations they find themselves in, citing many historical examples to illustrate his point. Zimbardo details his 1971 Stanford prison experiment, where ordinary volunteers playing guards in a mock prison rapidly became abusive. But he also describes the tortures committed by US army personnel in Iraq's Abu Ghraib prison in 2003—and how he himself testified in defence of one of those guards. committed by US army personnel in Iraq's Abu Ghraib prison in 2003—and how he himself testified in defence of one of those guards.

Macat analyses are available from all good bookshops and libraries.

Access hundreds of analyses through one, multimedia tool.
Join free for one month **library.macat.com**

Macat Pairs

Analyse historical and modern issues from opposite sides of an argument. Pairs include:

HOW WE RELATE TO EACH OTHER AND SOCIETY

Jean-Jacques Rousseau's
The Social Contract

Rousseau's famous work sets out the radical concept of the 'social contract': a give-and-take relationship between individual freedom and social order.

If people are free to do as they like, governed only by their own sense of justice, they are also vulnerable to chaos and violence. To avoid this, Rousseau proposes, they should agree to give up some freedom to benefit from the protection of social and political organization. But this deal is only just if societies are led by the collective needs and desires of the people, and able to control the private interests of individuals. For Rousseau, the only legitimate form of government is rule by the people.

Robert D. Putnam's
Bowling Alone

In *Bowling Alone*, Robert Putnam argues that Americans have become disconnected from one another and from the institutions of their common life, and investigates the consequences of this change.

Looking at a range of indicators, from membership in formal organizations to the number of invitations being extended to informal dinner parties, Putnam demonstrates that Americans are interacting less and creating less "social capital" – with potentially disastrous implications for their society.

It would be difficult to overstate the impact of *Bowling Alone*, one of the most frequently cited social science publications of the last half-century.

Printed in the United States
by Baker & Taylor Publisher Services